MANAGING LIKE A BOSS
Develop Yourself into a Leader

MANAGING LIKE A BOSS
Develop Yourself into a Leader

LES J. GOODWIN

For further information go to: ISEAdvisoryGroup.com

ISBN 978-0-9970972-0-7

Print management by Burnett Print Group, LLC, Los Angeles.
Printed and bound in China.

Library of Congress Control Number: 2015920280

10 9 8 7 6 5 4 3 2 1

DEDICATION

I want to thank all of the people who supported me in all aspects of my development as a Business Manager. Life is full of ups and downs and lessons of every kind, but the people who cared for me have always helped me stay the course.

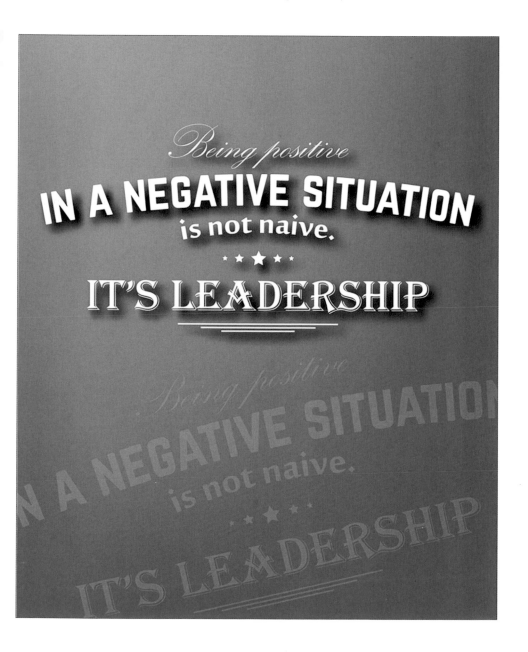

CONTENTS

PREFACE

It's my belief that OPPORTUNITY, EXPOSURE, and MENTORSHIP create a formula for LEADERSHIP, which is the only route to a successful business, *and* to a proud LEGACY for the "boss".

But the following chapters are more of a musing than a formula. They are a collection of articles I wrote and posted in 2015 in an attempt to bring more awareness to all the different aspects of being in charge. Having just recently retired, I felt a desire to look back over the course of my career in corporate America and share what I'd learned about Business Management, from the new perspective of being my *own* boss. I am not really laying out steps or a program to follow, but I'm touching on a few of the topics that I feel you will need to learn more about, using stories from my own life to illustrate those concepts, and hopefully, inspiring you to think and take action to further foster your success.

By presenting my thoughts on OPPORTUNITY, EXPOSURE, and MENTORSHIP, I am priming you with all the tools for great LEADERSHIP— but I am open to pushback and criticism on my ideas. I confess, I myself do not possess all the traits I emphasize here, but by becoming aware of them in myself and others over the years, I know I was able to develop a positive LEGACY at my company.

You don't need to be an actual boss, or even want to be one, to read this book and get something from it. This information will also help people who work *for* others to better understand the differences in the training and approach of many Managers. Personally, I was always more the type of employee to want to make my bosses look good, than to want to rise the ranks to become the "big boss" myself. This was my elective choice: to remain under strong leaders and to learn more and more from each of them. In truth, I have learned more under bad bosses than under good ones, as you'll see from many my stories. They pushed me beyond my abilities to perform at levels that surprised me. We all know that life has its own plans for each of us, and we must take responsibility for our careers, regardless of whether we work for a dream boss, or a petty micromanager. I *did* try to focus here on the importance of self-improvement—you can, in any position, become a solid, people-caring, and *honest* leader who inspires people to fulfill their dreams.

Again, for those of you who aren't striving to be the boss—just a more aware employee—this book should help you better assess the people you work for, allowing you to determine the level of respect, loyalty, commitment, and **trust** you might have in following them. For those of you who are already in management, or who want to become the most effective bosses possible, I challenge you to read this book with an open heart and mind. Challenge yourself! It isn't about agreeing with me or not; it's about you being willing to question your past communications, reactions, and other behaviors in order to become the best boss you can be.

I also need to thank all of the wonderful bosses, mentors, staff, and friends who supported me over the decades to help me rise in my career where I wanted to, allowing me to be forthright with my decisions, and giving me the devotion of their aid. A special thanks to my co-writer, Shannon Constantine Logan; to our editor, Madeline Schussel; to our designer Dana Marotta-Russo; and to Marcia Mosko of Burnett Print Group, LLC for helping me to make this book happen. These women brought talent, insight, and dedication to shape my writing, and my thought-processes. I am truly blessed to have had their help.

Please, enjoy this book. It is my dream that bringing these challenging topics to your attention will make a positive difference in your life, and in the lives of those you interact with—especially at work. I hope especially that women and people belonging to an ethnic minority who read this will see it as a guide to finding success in business, in spite of the many obstacles before them. The obstacles may not go away any time soon, but your awareness of how to play the game of business by developing a sturdy game plan should give you a better chance. With any lot in life, we can learn how to bring the best aspects of ourselves to our work, and how to become visible as worthy to those who can advance us.

Whoever you are, always look to your own passions and follow them; if you ever find you've lost your way, make a move to change. Don't be afraid to reinvent your career, or to help yourself or your boss to become a better leader. Without passion for what we do, we can have no hope or strength to continue doing it.

MANAGING LIKE A BOSS
Develop Yourself into a Leader

PART ONE

Opportunity

Seize the Opportunity to Change Your Business, Your People, and Yourself

CHAPTER ONE

Getting It Done through Project Management

A great opportunity to develop yourself into a leader presents itself with the very first project you are called upon to manage. In truth, this will be your startup challenge in managing major *changes*—to your business, to your colleagues and employees, and to your own leadership style. Knowing how to structure and put in place a process, and then to *own* the completion of a project, is key to meeting deadlines and budgets; this, in turn, is key to the success of your company. As you'll see in the three chapters that follow this one, it doesn't matter what type of management you're doing or what type of manager you are—no one can get the job done, and get it done well, without strong Project Management skills.

My goal in this chapter is to open your awareness to the multitude of ways that a Project Manager—and at times, your proper support of him or her—brings the likelihood of success to projects. Before we dive in, let me offer a simple definition of **Project Management**: it is the activity of planning, motivating, and controlling resources and procedures in order to achieve a specific goal. What a Project Manager does is divide his/her attention between tasks and teams or individuals, while monitoring interactions, financials, progress, and the overarching dynamics of Change Management (which we'll explore more in Chapter 2).

Project Managers can come from all different areas of a business—they could be internal Analysts, or they could Practitioners from the Operations or Technology departments. They could be moving up in their careers to Chief Operating Officers or Senior Management roles. In preparation, any of these people can take Project Management courses at online universities, or through other specialized training programs. (Most of the Project Managers I've interacted with were trained in "Six Sigma" methodology from General Electric.)

Strangely, my background as an Executive was void of any Project Management skills until much later in my career, and I wish I had stumbled into having these years earlier. I never did get formal training in this area, but I was eventually blessed to work with several (and one very special) highly-disciplined and seasoned Project Managers. I am incredibly grateful to them for enlightening me on the different aspects of their processes, which helped me learn to better organize and structure my own business plans.

Let me tell you the story of one particularly memorable Project Manager who I had the pleasure of working with. We were updating an older website for one of our departments, and the project was tricky because, on top of the feature improvements the company wanted, we had the added pressure of needing the website to conform to the company's protocols for security and reliability. As an Executive Manager, I tasked my Manager to collaborate with two other Department Managers to get an assessment together for the project. While I promised my Manager enough financial support, I wanted to make sure we had the resources and commitment to get it done in a cost-efficient and timely manner.

When the assessment was presented, I agreed to move forward with the project. The two Department Managers had assigned a Project Manager to prepare a plan for completing the website. I hadn't yet met her, but as it turned out, she was very detail-oriented and had strong people skills (more on this killer combo in Chapter 3). The countless hours they had all worked on scoping out, designing, testing the functionality of, and even picking pictures for the website was tremendous.

Early on, the Project Manager was getting some pressure from her Department Manager to get me to sign the project document, which would certify my promised financial commitment (since we'd only made a verbal agreement so far). I'd received the document, but I had been too busy to sign and return it. Despite several reminders from my assistant—prompted by the Project Manager—it had sat on my desk for days, and worse, I kept forgetting to return the Project Manager's call.

This is when the resourcefulness of this manager really took the spotlight. She orchestrated a last-minute face-to-face meeting through my assistant to get me to sign the damn document. My assistant literally came to my door, told me I had a guest, and as fast as that, the Project Manager made her way into my office and walked up to my desk with the document. Although I hadn't met her yet, I immediately knew who she was and what this was about. I said, "Let me see it." Then I turned to the signature page and signed it. I'd reviewed it earlier, so I already knew the details.

What she didn't know was that my Manager, who spoke very highly of her, had been encouraging me to meet her. Here was the perfect opportunity for me to watch her in action, dealing with a difficult manager: me. This Project Manager was known as the "soft hammer" because she had perseverance, and she would push you to do something, but you couldn't *feel* it. There was no retreat in her, but she never rubbed people the wrong way. Later, when we'd gotten to know each other better, she confessed she thought I was a jerk at the time. I simply thought her tactics were surprisingly effective. To this day, we laugh about it.

Her presentations to the group (I would barge in from time to time) were always well prepared, focused on the results, and delivered with a smile of confidence. All eyes are always on the Project Manager, and one of the most important traits he or she can possess is to never let anyone see fear. If a Project Manager loses the confidence, respect, and loyalty of employees and/or superiors, the entire project can be lost.

It's worth reiterating that **people skills** are key to the success of a Project Manager. All the training and discipline in the world will be a complete waste if good social qualities are not exhibited. The Project Manager on the web project had this art in spades.

The new website turned out to be a success; we finished early and under budget, thanks very much to our Project Manager. Had we not had someone with the same professional ability to perform under pressure—and to take pride in finishing the project—it might not have been accomplished.

Managing Project Managers

But this chapter probably won't teach you how to be a good Project Manager; there are tons of resources online for that. More interesting to me are the ways that you can be more aware during the process of *dealing with* Project Managers from the ranks above. To pull your weight—and to learn your own essential management lessons—here are several questions that you might ask yourself when preparing to interact with a Project Manager:

• Can I explain the project vision? How can I expect a good plan if I cannot explain the end product?

• Have I remembered that timing and other expectations are critical? Time is money and the transformation process is laden with possible delays and changes.

• Are my people reliable, competent, and available? Project Managers have a unique knowledge of the capabilities of individuals and can tell me whether I have what I need to succeed.

• Does my staff understand the necessity of having a Project Manager? If not, I must train and educate them to participate, and not hinder, our projects.

• Am *I* an obstacle to the Project Management process? My style of management and my *own* people skills play a large factor. It all starts at the top.

• Am I delegating enough? Holding on to every detail will hinder the process.

Knowing when to introduce a Project Manager into the process is also essential; it's best to bring him/her in right from the start.

During my 36-year banking career, I've been involved with many acquisitions. Early in my career, I worked for a large 40-plus branch bank that grew through acquisition 'projects', and I observed the effects of poor execution so many times, I lost count. This bank's poor communication and ineffective Change-Management Plans clearly had an impact on employees and customers, as well as on operational integration.

Later in my career, with a larger bank, I watched as the company bought 40 branches from an even larger national bank. Fortunately, the structure of this acquisition was more planned out than those at my previous company had been, and the staff we acquired had more experience than we did at my current bank. We still lacked much-needed Project Managers on our end, but the larger bank had enough expertise to craft an effective Communication Plan to help the process along.

Much later, that same bank finally engaged the expertise of Project Managers to implement and guide the changes needed to complete its acquisitions. It created a Project Management Office (PMO), and what a difference it made! The hours of research, planning, conference calls, and countless revisions the office handled—I was glad to be on the outside, but even gladder it existed, at last. It was like watching Grand Central Station. No matter who you were—a Practitioner or a Strategist, a Staff Manager or an Executive—you were aided by the PMO. I had gotten a taste of its processes from some earlier projects at the company, but I'd never seen anything handled so well as this. The PMO independently fought a full-scale war—with the bank's reputation on the line—against both government and internal financial timelines, in order to complete acquisitions with as few customer casualties as possible.

There are so many projects that require Project Management methodology; they don't have to be big, expansive undertakings, like acquisitions. I've learned a lot about participating and cooperating with Project Managers on smaller projects, too. When you're helping a Project Manager, whether you're a support person or a manager yourself, you have to understand your role. If you're staying reliable, engaged, and relevant, then you are adding value, and a Project Manager will communicate this up to Executive Management (whether that's you or someone above you both). Likewise, if you don't understand what role you play, or if it looks like you're just barely showing up, then you aren't bringing value, and your failed efforts will also get communicated to your bosses. On a project of any size, you must be prepared to make management easier for everyone.

I always say to bring your "A" game when you go into a meeting with Project Management. They are expecting it, and they can easily see when you're not giving things your best effort. Upper Management frequently asks Project Managers for feedback as to whether all participants seem engaged. Remember, this is ultimately about money. Don't waste the company's resources.

It is easy for you or someone above you to negatively affect a project by adjusting the process midstream—perhaps, derailing it due to another, undisclosed agenda. I am referring to the times when a hidden motivator like pride, arrogance, greed, or incompetence distorts the Project Management process, resulting in poor decisions and, ultimately, a failed project.

At the end of my banking career, as an Executive, I witnessed one of these interferences playing out during an acquisition. My own staff, the Strategy Department, the Project Managers, and the other internal teams had all embraced the process from the very beginning, moving forward with excitement about increasing our profitability and sustainability. Even with this fortuitous start, power struggles among the Executives loomed and inevitably interfered, causing unforeseen delays and distractions.

In this scenario, you can detect a hidden agenda if you're watching for one. When there seems to be a lack of open communication or transparency from the Executives, there are often backdoor adjustments and compromises being made in which people who are left unaware will be directly affected. The Project Manager will then be confounded by erratic communications from above and have to constantly readjust the expectations of the group. These types of distractions cost the project a great deal in the loss of valuable opportunities, productivity, time, and money, too. Equally bad, they take resources away from other important projects and cause deep frustration within the organization as a whole.

On another project, years prior, Executives used a "Go Between" person to act on behalf of them in order to sway the project without being directly or visibly involved. Talk about hidden agendas! This "Go Between" asked me to consider advancing a strategic plan to expand into a new market segment. The original plan had budgeted for several staff and a manager, and the Executives were really just trying to sidetrack us while a new budget cycle approached in which they could 'realign' (fire and hire) that staff.

So, one day, the "Go Between" came into my office to talk about the newer initiative. Within seconds of him speaking, I heard a little voice in my head saying, "They're trying to alter the timing and resources of the plan." He suggested I dilute the group's efficiency by making an existing manager and two staff multitask, instead of hiring the requisite additional people. The "Go Between" wasn't a business manager, so I knew the message was actually coming from the Big Boss. I sat back and listened, and when he had finished, I said, "Go back and tell her no."

"I will not proceed in that direction without a fully focused team. We will not move forward until it's all ready to be executed as we originally planned."

I was known for my pushback, but he knew that I was just calling it as I saw it. *All* of the initiatives on the table had to be considered relative to one another in terms of dividing up resources. Picking the right time to execute each project was vital. Often, we all go after the same resources at the same time, overusing them, burning them out, and forcing all missions to get scaled back impossibly.

KEYS TO SUCCESS 🔑 *Chapter 1 Review*

- **Project Management** is the activity of planning, motivating, and controlling resources and procedures in order to achieve a specific goal. Whether you *are*, you are *overseeing*, or you are working *for* a Project Manager, you need to be able to hold yourself accountable for your specific contribution to the project.

- First, get a survey of your staff and support **resources**, keeping an eye out for hidden issues or concerns. There are often weak spots overlooked at the outset, usually because we neglected to ask about them.

- All projects require adjustment. Make sure you are ready for **change**!

- Ask yourself if you are open to learning the process, and to figuring out *when* and *how* you'll be adding **value**. If I'm on the project, I know I am needed—but I need to also know my place.

- You must see your part in the **bigger picture**. Don't come in with a narrow view.

- Are you willing to attend meetings to talk through the important steps? So many people miss the **conversations** that were crucial in helping to move things forward.

- Always ask your staff to participate in the project, even if they are not key players. It'll be a great development **opportunity** for them, too! If they cannot participate, you should offer to teach them what you learn.

- Get ready to manage **expectations**—your own, and those of others you are responsible for. There are so many unknowns and uncertainties. Expectations must be formed, be they good or bad.

- Above all, start practicing good **people skills** during your interactions with (or as) a Project Manager. It's likely there will be many who *won't*, so you *have* to do your part in this area.

I hope this chapter has expanded your awareness of the importance of Project Management. I challenge you to clearly recognize the value Project Management adds to any business, and to use it to maximize your opportunities to accomplish great feats.

CHAPTER TWO

Why Change Management is About People

Change does not come easily, as many of you already know. There are countless books on the topic of change, and there is no formal training on how to master it. But as a seasoned—and retired—practitioner of the art of implementing large-scale structural changes in the business world, I know that mastering this process plays a vital role in the future success of any company.

"**Change Management**" is roughly defined as the process of transforming individuals, teams, and organizations into a future state. There are several issues that can cause a company to initiate Change Management, including a move at the top (such as the loss or addition of an Executive), some other form of corporate reshuffling, a governmental or regulatory shift, economic fluctuations (like a recession), or even environmental or social factors that are affecting a certain marketplace. Sometimes it's a **crisis**, like when there's an urgent need to create more revenue, or when the core team's performance has failed to deliver an expected result. Other times, companies just **evolve** and expand and find that, over the years, they need to redefine what they do or how they do it, including reassessing current employees to see who fits their future needs. In any of these cases, companies must reevaluate their paradigms and begin to catalyze change.

In any of these cases, changing a company's business model deeply and directly affects *people*—and their jobs. This effect tends to be more severe than it can be under mere Project Management, when sometimes, job-related changes occur in the pursuit of one particular goal. Still, if someone has mastered Project Management, it is likely he or she will be able to execute a Change-Management Communication Plan that better appeals to the people in transition.

Successful changes at work, whether on a project or on the entire infrastructure, have a lot to do with **trust**; the employees, managers, and owners all have to "buy in" to a vision and believe that the company is headed in the right direction. This starts with a trust of leadership at the very top, which depends largely upon how these leaders lay out a Change-Management Communication Plan. More than once in my career, I've caught glimpse of a great vision from my higher-ups, but have heard no clear word of a Change-Management strategy on how to implement the vision successfully. In an instance like this, it's almost as if leadership alone trusts that passion for the vision will carry the way, without considering in advance the changes the company will have to undergo. Of course, the size and maturity of an organization play roles in its ability to effectively execute a new vision, but an awareness at the outset of how the status quo will be reshaped is even more critical.

Trust has to be established *beyond* the passion of the leadership. From the very beginning, from the top down, trust has to be fostered in *the concept of change*. If implemented correctly, this thinking will have a rippling positive effect throughout the company, saving time and money later on.

Crisis Management

Early in my career as a manager, I was tasked with taking over operational responsibility for a three-branch bank in a remote, tourist-heavy section of the central coast of California. It was very isolated from other branches—and from headquarters—which allowed it to be managed differently than the other banks in the network. But previously, this had led to disastrous results. The three branches had just been through a witch-hunt to remove any management remaining from before their acquisition years ago, and also, through a rigorous internal audit of compliance with system-wide policies and procedures. The audit came back with over 300 exceptions (normally a branch would get 3 to 10, but 300 was unheard of). The branches were rated as unsatisfactory and immediately reported to the Board of Directors.

That was where I came in. I was asked by our bank's upper management to visit the branches and interview the staff just before the close of the audit. I was then ordered to fire the current Head of Operations before sitting through the final audit reading. The meeting was long and demoralizing, and the auditors made sure they pointed out which persons they felt were responsible for the errors. With so much blame cast, morale had all but disintegrated.

The real shame was that in my meetings with branch staff, I had found that most of them seemed honest and hardworking. There were some young staff members trying hard to start their careers in a small city, and those who were not as young had come with ample experience from other banks. The customers loved these branches and their employees—there was trust there—so any performance issues were strictly internal. After removing the Head of Operations, my assessment was that the remaining staff and management team shared the passion to do a better job and the know-how to avoid a repeat of the downfall.

Based on my recommendations, we immediately put **Crisis Management** into effect. Headquarters asked me to take on the role of Head of Operations for the three branches and to make whatever changes were necessary without negatively affecting the strong customer experience they'd already established. It was clear that the staff would need to be educated on the policies and procedures of the bank, with ongoing compliance monitoring and stronger managerial oversight.

At the first general meeting I called as their new boss, I laid out the facts and discussed the current structural deficiencies—how they'd failed to meet the bank's standards. I then shared some personal past experiences related to this topic so they could see the future in a better light. I *didn't* cast blame, and I didn't drag out any of their old skeletons to beat on them. Then I shared the plan: we needed several types of changes, and it would be best to tackle them in 15 little bites, instead of trying to eat the entire elephant at once. Setting expectations for your staff is important; also, showing them patience and a long view of what they'll accomplish reassures them that you will be reasonable as they work to meet these expectations. You have to show them you know that, as they say, Rome wasn't built in a day.

One year after our meeting, almost to the date, the internal audits arrived to start their process again. The audit went quickly this time, because now, we were very prepared. By the end of it, we were told we had only three exceptions—for all three branches, combined. We had taken an orderly approach to making positive changes, and the result was a more confident working environment. The employees were so proud of their clean audit that even better customer service followed, as well.

Evolutional Management

There's a difference between Crisis Management (like the story I just told) and how a company deals with the natural "yin and yang" cycles that happen in any

business—the ups and downs. The questions of centralization, decentralization, growing or shrinking an organization, and the fluctuation of business risk for stable revenue can all come into play when management considers a major structural change called for by the simple passing of time. As I'll discuss in the next chapter, different elements and tools are needed at different times in the life cycle of a successful business. For now, we'll look at three different scenarios that might call for **Evolutional Management**.

In our first scenario, we see how Change Management can get *really* bad. I'm not just referring to poorly executed transitions, but to when change is used as a tool to distract from obvious misbehavior. There is a certain management style wherein people with less than honorable intentions like to foster a state of flux (i.e. chaos). The employees are so confused that nobody notices what's in front of them, which can be performance issues, incompetence, or even fraud.

When I was 30 years old, the Board of Directors and Banking Regulators of a failing Thrift and Loan in Southern California asked me to take the role of acting President and CEO. The former President had been using loan portfolio sales and a bank acquisition to distract everyone from the core issues: a fraudulent equipment lease portfolio and inappropriate accounting. Acquisitions are needed for a company to grow, so it temporarily creates false excitement. After a brief assessment, I realized that nobody on the team knew enough about acquisitions or loan sales to see beyond the snow job the President had given them. (He was a smart man, and he could out-talk anyone.) Of course, at last, the bottom fell out.

After the fraud was discovered, there were plans to survive, but the hole was too deep, and the Thrift and Loan moved from a survival strategy to a liquidation plan in less than six months. My employees had started out with an aura of general excitement and relief, and had arrived at "Shit! We don't have jobs anymore." At first, the dream of survival gives momentum to necessary changes, but when you're in liquidation mode, dispersing fear becomes the main focus. So different are the dynamics of the two modes, in fact, that changing my approach to managing here was a Change Management challenge unto itself. It was now my job to motivate the remaining staff to stay long enough to reduce the loss to shareholders and regulators, a task that was so astoundingly difficult I had enough material for a whole book—*A View from the Vault*—that regales my misadventures here.

In a less heated scenario, Evolutional Change doesn't involve recovering from a blatant fraud, but from something subtler—like managerial incompetence. When this is happening, employees burn out fast. Good people may get frustrated and leave their jobs or get themselves fired. Others will fill in their gaps, taking on excess responsibilities during changeovers and delivering watered-down performances. Any way you look at it, change motivated by managerial inadequacy is detrimental for the people in your company.

You also have to consider the impact Evolutional Management has on customers and suppliers. Remember, people like consistency, and when an organization seems to be shifting, uncertainty can creep into these relationships and affect customer loyalty. A good book to read that I discovered later in my career is *The Ultimate Question* by Fred Reichheld and Rob Markey— it addresses Change Management, Customer Relations, and Revenue and offers a disciplined approach to success in these areas.

A third common Evolutional scenario occurs after management has succeeded in effecting a new paradigm, but when they don't know how to manage their teams differently to accommodate the change. It's easy to slip back into old styles, but what worked in the past probably won't work in this new future. For example, at a company I once worked for, I watched one of our Senior

Managers get promoted to an Executive Manager during a large structural shift in the company. He was an ambitious man, and as management was weeding out the staff, he had naturally come up for a coveted position. This man had used proven tactics to get himself ahead in business; he had bullied his way to the top. He was the type to bug you every day, and to demand he be at every meeting with every prospect and every customer. He was also a classic **micromanager**. (More on this topic in Chapters 3 and 7.)

The people skills he needed in this Change Management case were nonexistent, and as the staff scrambled to include him on everything they did, Senior Executive Management grew more and more disappointed at not seeing him realize the strategic vision expected of him at this level.

"What if, and I know this sounds kooky, we communicated with the employees."

Changes at the managerial level are Change Management *events*. There is always a dynamic transition for everyone involved, and without a disciplined Change Management Plan, the rippling effects can delay progress—or, as in this worst-case scenario, they can cause managers to lose the respect and support they need from both below *and* above in order to transition successfully.

Change Management is a daunting task for anyone in any circumstance. It can seem effortless when it is done correctly, but it is never without complications. The moral here is that if the organization changes, so must you!

KEYS TO SUCCESS 🔑 *Chapter 2 Review*

- **Change Management** is necessary in an earth-shattering situation (**Crisis Management**) or simply at moments in the life cycle of any business (**Evolutional Management**)—but even in the natural course of management and mismanagement, change is a challenge!

- The uppermost leadership has to do more than inspire a *passion* for change. He/she must have a **Communication Plan** for the *vision* that's being implemented. This is the only way to establish and maintain the most important factor: <u>trust</u>.

- If change is required, it is imperative that the management and staff at all levels have the skills *and the perspectives* needed to accomplish the goal. Assess the whole team before diving in. Success is dependent upon a secure **evaluation** of your employees' roles, and of how you see them evolving into the future paradigm.

- **Buy-in** at all levels of the company requires **intense personal interaction** in an effort to help employees understand and commit to change. It is impossible to get 100% buy-in, but even 95% can create a successful movement.

- Being upfront and *not casting blame* or beating any old skeletons sets the standard for moving forward. The challenge is not to forget the past, which contains valuable lessons, but to make sure you do not *live* in the past. **Understand the past** and the reasons why change is necessary.

- Make sure you have one-on-one sessions and small group meetings with your staff, and properly lay the groundwork. Set accountability milestones and an end date for the change to help them **get a glimpse of the future**. (People want to know when they will "get there".)

- Hope and security is important to your employees, but there will always be a displacement of people during Change Management. Don't just focus on the numbers. This can be difficult in the face of financial needs, but always take into consideration **the dynamics** of your *employees, customers, and vendors* during the transition.

- Stay flexible. Be willing to change midstream if necessary, and to adjust for the unforeseen. **Not all changes are good.** So don't be in a rush. Commit to the *long haul* of change; it took you years to get this far, and it will take you years to get even farther.

CHAPTER THREE

The Difference between Micromanagement and Detail-Oriented Management

My entire career, I've heard that "**micromanagement**" is bad. In forty years under other managers, and as a manager myself, I have never heard the term used in a positive context. Many articles have been written on the topic examining the pros and cons—but mostly the cons. Even a quick search on Google or Wikipedia will tell you that it generally has a negative connotation. Now, I am no Micromanagement Expert—I am just a corporate veteran with many battle stories to tell about every type of management style there is. It is my belief that micromanagement is, indeed, unhealthy, but that **detail-oriented management**—a related style—has gotten a bad rap.

I spent 36 years working my way up the corporate ladder in banking, but my career *started* at Sears in the 70s. Sears was well established (it had been around for 122 years), and even with the stiff competition from JCPenney, Montgomery Ward, and the up-and-coming FedCo, Sears was considered *the* place to work. I worked in three stores during my short time with them, each unique, yet similar. The first store was in Covina; the second was in La Puente at the new Puente Hills Mall—a large, modern store with younger employees, but with the same traditional Sears pride and mystique as the others; and the third was in Bakersfield, when I transferred to a local store to work part-time during college. Back then, I was active in sports, and I needed flexible hours to accommodate my daily workouts and travel schedule. I mostly worked weekends, and a couple of nights a week.

Sears had an excellent management-training program, where regional headquarters would hand-select and advance Department Managers who they felt could soon hold higher leadership roles and run the stores. The pride of Sears shown through its employees. Under members of the program, I got my first real view of management, up front and personal. As part of their training, I worked under three of the five managers in the program at my store: one woman and two men. They rotated between departments and would often ask me to work in their sections, which allowed me to see different aspects of the business. My favorite manager was Mr. Jenkins. He was a solid leader, and you could tell that he cared. Out of the five people in the program, he was clearly one of the top two. He also had a little edge to him, which I thought was probably due to the fact that he knew he had to prove himself as one of the few black managers in the region.

I mention gender and ethnicity for two reasons: (1) because it was the 70s, when such 'mixtures' in the workplace were even more deliberate—and even more challenging—than they are today, and (2) because these politics had *always* struck a strong chord with me. As a child, I was an Air Force brat, and I was often moved around from city to city. We lived in Alabama during the early 60s, and then in minority-heavy cities in Southern California, where I attended predominantly black and Hispanic schools as a young white boy. This showed me the scars that many carried, and it gave me a clearer view of sex and race discrimination. It's hard to know the emotions of others, but I did notice that minority groups had a different lot in life, and often, a different view because of it.

Mr. Jenkins showed me the ropes, and even went out of his way to introduce me to the General Manager. Leslie (same name as mine!) was a Sears's veteran, and he carried his leadership qualities in his impeccable appearance. He was a tall, stoic man, definitely the "Captain" of the ship, but still very warm and charming. This was his store—the high revenue store. Apparently, his mentorship was so sought after that there were many managers in the training program seeking to work under him. I sensed his importance at the time, but now, many years later, I can really see the brilliance of his management style, and his effectiveness at motivating people.

This brings me to my first taste of micromanagement vs. detail-oriented management. It was clear that Leslie knew the operations of the entire store inside and out. When he discussed a department's performance with my direct bosses, I could tell he knew every fact, but wasn't revealing everything that he knew. He took his time, and let the managers reveal the truth about the department's performance through the conversation. I respected his approach. Many of the managers were responsive to it, and joined him in taking the details very seriously. This way, his managers learned faster, and didn't feel beaten down for the things they didn't know yet.

Each of my three direct managers took a slightly *different* approach to running the departments, and each had a varying degree of people skills (not everyone is blessed with those necessary for good management). I believe that your childhood and transition into adulthood factor into your management style, because my first impression was that those managers who fought with emotional issues like insecurity, immaturity, or lack of personal discipline were the 'typical' micromanagers. (I struggled with some of these same issues, so I knew them well and could spot them in others easily.)

As I mentioned, the managers in the Sears training program were learning the ropes of running a store, but they were also being evaluated on how they treated the people under their supervision. How a manager motivated his/her employees, or relied on them for information, was taken into consideration. The effectiveness of both skill sets weighed heavily in the program. I learned to tell a good, detail-oriented manager from a bad micromanager by the difference in the way they viewed people. Generally, a good manager focused on promoting the team members and team loyalty, and a bad manager saw people as having little value in the long-term—their employees were more like slaves.

The experiences you have under a micromanager force you to learn skills that move you faster along on the curve, but the price you pay in terms of stress and isolation is steep. People working under micromanagers tended to wash out fast. Also, as we'll explore in Part III, those people then lacked the mentoring they would have needed to become more competent, confident, and functional as employees.

The way the employees acted under each of the five Sears Department Managers told me which managers had the ability to be on top of the details without driving everyone crazy in the process. The good managers revealed themselves as leaders by creating an open forum and exercising healthy follow-up skills, and employee performance excelled as a result. The micromanagers pushed their employees to get things done so that they didn't have to feel like they were doing everything, and morale beneath them plummeted.

Early in my banking career, I was fortunate to be the first candidate in another management-training program at a small community bank with over 30 branches in the San Joaquin Valley. This program not only showed me the aspects of running a bank, but it also allowed me to continue to observe different management styles and the effectiveness of each as it related to employee performance and personal reputation.

After a year in training, Senior Management allowed me to attend a course at UC Santa Barbara called the Management and Supervisory Development Program. The instructor, Howard Wilson, taught more than 500,000 people, including 8,000 managers at 800 companies, during the conference. He had my full attention. I was still young back then, so to me, he seemed to be 100 years old, but the issues he spoke about were relevant for anyone at any age. The topics he covered were: transitioning to supervisor, motivation, improving supervisory skills, changing behavior, communication, counseling, training and development, time effectiveness, and understanding yourself. He hit all of the vital subjects.

I thank God for this experience because I've used every single one of the skills I learned from that program for the rest of my corporate career, and I have continued to mentor others based on this same knowledge.

I learned that all good management starts with communication, a basic building block that so many neglect to use properly. The ability to learn the dynamics of conversation and to listen first and foremost elicits better responses from both parties. This allows others to feel that they are part of the solution. Empowerment (many people use this word, but don't know how to practice it) gives people under the management structure the ability to communicate "up" about issues and problems, and about their suggestions for fixing them. A micromanager would rather tell people what to do, or chastise them for incompetence, than listen to them or allow them to participate in the problem solving.

The Seasons

I also learned that agreements between a manager and his/her staff must change based on various job assignments and on the work environment—startup, maintenance, crisis, and (of course) "cover your ass" mode. Different circumstances cause differing levels of stress and/or threat, which, in turn, alter expectations. I like to think of these work environments as seasons, because they all have a beginning and an end; nothing lasts forever.

In a leadership-training program later in life, I learned a concept that embodied these 'seasons'. A timeline of the evolution of a business was laid out like an elongated Yin-and-Yang symbol, an infinity loop that had highs and lows. The lesson was that if you don't know where you are in the loop, you cannot manage any volatility, and you cannot succeed. Another way of putting it is that history repeats itself. Knowing the history of your business, learning from it, and having a vision to be more successful in the future creates a sustainable working environment, in spite of its necessary ebb and flow.

In a hostile season under a micromanager, you cannot free yourself easily from a canopy of poor behavior—but if you're competent and know what to expect, there can be some relief. You must never lose sight of the fact that you have value, even though you are being seen or treated otherwise. (Of course, I have also had to learn this lesson the hard way, but I am a quick study, and I rarely reenter a truly bad scenario.) I have seen many unprepared people face a micromanager and get their asses handed to them. I hate watching people be scolded, but I have always thought those people should have played the game better.

Learn to Play, in Any Weather

I don't have much tolerance for people who seem not know the social dynamics at hand, or who just aren't trained or prepared with a plan. Worse, what is that saying? *"Ignorance is not knowing. Stupidity is knowing and doing it anyway."* I'm not writing to be politically correct here, I'm trying to make a point: there's no excuse not to learn what you need to know about dealing with people, so there's no need to be guilty of the former. If you *do* learn and still can't treat your employees well—well, then, you're guilty of the latter. All the same, you're the only one to blame if you can't learn to survive even the stupidest micromanager.

I remember getting a call from a past employee who had washed out in one of my departments; she had been a young, naïve woman, and her direct boss had been ruthlessly demanding. Four years after we had worked together, she was asking me to lunch. While I didn't know the exact nature of her call, I felt I needed to accept the invitation.

During our meal, she told me that she was finally ready to play the game. She explained that after she had left, she'd learned better work skills and was more mature. She was determined to perform at a higher level. I was so shocked and impressed. She had already progressed to a middle-management position at another company, and I could tell she had now learned the elements of being an effective manager by how she spoke about her people. In part, she'd used her past micromanager boss as an example of what *not* to do, and she'd worked very hard since then to improve herself.

She knew that management at the top of my group was good, and that her past boss had been an inherited issue; she didn't blame me for it. I told her I was proud of her and that despite our limited interactions prior to this moment, we must have laid a path of good faith to this eventual meeting.

I used to joke with my staff and friends by saying, *"I'm a micromanager, but you would never know it. I'm not really interested in the details—just the thoughts and passion behind the actions, and your results."* I did this to stimulate discussion about management styles. I was never actually seen as a micromanager, so it always created a conversation.

Of course, I *did* always look at the details (the numbers) and circle back with employees if I found anything interesting, or disappointing, in their performances—that's just standard delegation and follow up. But what I often found really exciting was when my staff would give me suggestions or challenge me to make changes. This told me that there was trust established and no fear of repercussion, and that they could watch out and find fixes for issues I didn't even know existed. They were motivated simply by loyalty, pride, and the passion to do a great job—to not let me down.

Leadership Starts at the Top

People will drift to their own demise, I've found, if you don't set your expectations clearly. In my last corporate job, I was in charge of development and retention of both corporate and commercial customers. If I didn't set the expectations high for sales and for customer service, I knew I'd be doing everyone a disservice. No matter what, the main party to blame when there are performance issues is always management—this includes me. We, managers, should be held to a different standard.

Later in my career, as I moved up in banking and got closer to the Executives, with their inflated egos and lower tolerance for risk, the management game changed. With my sports background, I see organizations like athletic teams—everyone has their positions and must have the passion to compete and to win. At this new level, it was more like a veiled polo match than a fun football scrimmage. Executive Managers appeared more polished (though not in all cases) and seemed to use politics to get things done—in many cases, with more benefit to themselves than to the organization or its customers. After all these years, my assessment is that 20% of managers actually have great people skills and rely on them to be successful, while the other 80% got to their positions by taking out those around them. (I'm sure I just pissed off the 80%, but that really is how I see it.)

Towards the end of my corporate banking career, I found it hard not to act out towards those bosses I felt had poor people skills. I even remember showing one of them an assessment of me from a leadership-development program that suggested I was passive aggressive, explaining that we both should be aware of my tendency in order to have the best possible working relationship. Knowing is better than not knowing; I don't want to be stupid!

But an insecure manager will always have problems dealing with strong people directly. From what I've observed, most micromanagers do not like confrontation, and they use others to carry out difficult personnel tasks. Weaker staff are thrown to the wolves and openly questioned and condemned in public. This produces fear of the bite, but ironically, this fear stops creativity and loyalty, which are key factors for success.

As a detail-oriented manager, despite my "passive-aggressive" diagnosis, I strive to be the complete opposite. If I gave you an assignment and it didn't work out, the next thing I'd be doing is sitting down with you face to face to have a candid discussion on how to either solve the issues or create a resolution to exit. It's never fun dealing with difficult people issues, but if you stick to the facts and make it your personal mission to do what is best for your employees, they will accept bad news—even harsh criticism—in a different frame of mind.

A micromanager will never take responsibility for what happened, and he or she will only ever blame others. Micromanagers are typically so short-sighted as to not see that their actions at the top have a direct impact on the performance of the people under their management.

As our world becomes more self-aware, treatment of people in the workplace appears in the papers and on the Internet more and more every day. Bad management is a serious business liability. The wasted revenues, resources, and talent, and the amount of lawsuits and bad reputations generated, should be enough of a determinate for you *not* to ignore the presence of micromanagers in your organization.

I am not saying we should fire or throw away all micromanagers, but that we should work alongside them and give them coaching. I have interviewed many people on the topic of mentoring (more in Part III), and I have found out that only about 20% of managers were actually coached properly. (This is, of course, consistent with my projection of the percentage of managers who have the right skills for the job.) Whenever I hired people from other departments or from competitors, I came to assume that they had had little to no mentoring before then. This made me tolerant of their relative ignorance, so it didn't bother me if the person made a mistake or two. When people make mistakes, both personally and in business, they look at life and responsibility differently after healing from their experiences. If people tell me they've never made a mistake, I'm sure they are either lying, or of little use to me. No one is perfect.

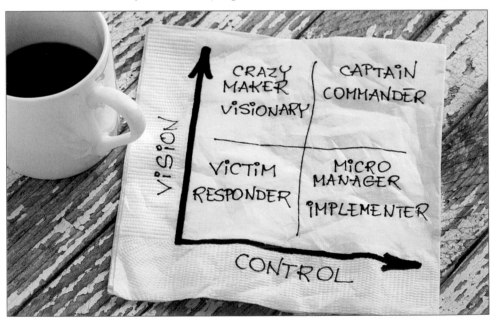

So I'm not simply trying to beat up on micromanagers who have bad people skills. I want to focus on developing the skills necessary for becoming a healthy, solid manager who knows the details of the company, and who also has the ability to motivate people to the fullest capacity. In my personal life, I've learned that if parents ("managers") do not seek therapy (training) to change their bad behaviors, and just keep blaming their kids ("staff"), they only perpetuate a dysfunctional family environment. Your business works in the exact same way.

KEYS TO SUCCESS 🔑 *Chapter 3 Review*

- **Micromanagement** is bad. **Detail-Oriented Management** is good! You can tell a micromanager from a detail-oriented manager by the difference in the way they view, motivate, and rely upon their employees: a bad manager handles people like *slaves*, while a good one is a *team player*.

- When managing **performance**, leadership shouldn't hold the facts over the heads of employees, whether employees know the facts or not. Good managers take their time in letting *truths reveal themselves* through gentle **delegation**, open **communication**, and **follow-up**.

- **People skills** are absolutely necessary for good management. Some people have them, and some people don't (or at least, not enough of them). Struggling with emotional issues like *insecurity, immaturity, or a lack of personal discipline* is a fast track to micromanagement, but *training, coaching, and mentoring* can ease this dysfunction.

- **Ignorance** is not understanding social dynamics, but **stupidity** is choosing not to learn about them (or, worse, choosing to ignore them). This applies to both perpetrators—and victims—of micromanagement. If you're going to play the game of business, you're going to have to survive the **seasons**—even those of stress and isolation—by taking as much **responsibility** as possible for yourself and your staff.

- The evolution of a business is an **infinity loop** with highs and lows, and thus, agreements between a manager and his/her staff are always in flux. You need to know where you are in the loop in order to succeed.

- It *should be exciting w*hen your staff wants *to c*hallenge you with suggestions. This is **empowerment**, and it means that <u>trust</u> has been established. Better yet, it means you now have an omnipresent eye on company issues. Employees aren't motivated by *fear of repercussion*, but by the freedom to be *creative*, by *loyalty* to you, and by the *pride* of doing a great job.

- **Leadership starts at the top**, so set your expectations clearly, and set them high. If your employees aren't performing well, make it your *personal mission* to do what is best for them. Remember that what matters are the *thoughts and passion* behind their actions, and their **results**.

If companies really want to inspire people to work for them and to work at their fullest potentials, leaders should address the micromanagement topic with vigor, providing coaching and mentorship to those in need. I wish prosperity for those who pursue healthy, functional, and fun workplaces! If Executives work on handling the bad seeds while encouraging growth for detail-oriented managers who truly care, they won't need my wish.

PART TWO

Exposure

Give and Gain Exposure to Kick-start Success

CHAPTER FOUR

The Difference Between Practitioners and Strategists

This chapter will outline some different styles of interaction between business Strategists and Practitioners. A **Practitioner** is a person who is actively engaged in and qualified for the act or discipline of a certain profession. A **Strategist** is a person who is skilled in formulating and implementing strategy.

Typically, Strategists lay out plans and goals, while Practitioners complete objectives. There are business-school programs focused solely on strategy, and often, accounting and consulting firms look for bright talent straight out of college. People must *elect* this career path in order to follow it, but once they do, they get immediate guidance and a wide scope of training from their employers.

Practitioners, on the other hand, often fall into their careers and learn management or trade skills as a result of their work. These practical skills are vital mainly to the businesses they are part of. For a Practitioner, it can take many years in the field to develop a strong skill-set, and sometimes, it grows out of a single, focused job, limited in scope.

I have found, however, that what one lacks in *breadth*, the other may lack in sheer *immersion*. Both are elements of **exposure**, and while many Strategists seem to make their way up their own food chain—often moving from firm to firm—it can be difficult for them to transition into permanent business manager roles, because they lack hands-on experience. On the other hand, Practitioners may move up in position within their businesses, but it can be difficult for them to broaden their applied knowledge beyond their current systems (to switch companies), or to learn multiple business strategies (to adapt to internal change).

But Practitioners and Strategists can work together, and they can both share in the success of achieving a goal! The differences in their perspectives on how to Project Manage, to determine the timing of events, and to deal with people can certainly vary dramatically. If you are in doubt as to which role you play, you should ask yourself whether you are more of a theorist (Strategist), or more of a manager (Practitioner).

Over the course of my 36-year banking career, I have primarily been a Practitioner. It wasn't until later in my career that I even interacted with Strategists, and I had to learn to collaborate with them in order to complete projects. In the course of my learning curve, I noticed many similarities in our approaches to guidelines, policies, and procedures; still, risk management and other monitoring tasks required some maneuvering for us to get on the same page. Central to our mastering communication about visions, plans, milestones, delays, and project completion was a thoughtfully subjective process of mutual review.

I have observed that Upper Management will tend to believe a Strategist over a Practitioner in the scoping process of almost any endeavor. Executives love that Strategists are able to explain multiple viewpoints. They are able to do this from an observational standpoint, due to their training in various industry practices. Strategists also tend to question…everything.

One of the downsides of being a Practitioner during the scoping phase of a project is not being able to effectively persuade Executive Management on how to get the job done. Practitioners are, as I've explained, sometimes seen as being single-minded, or as having limited views. As a result, while employees of a Practitioner may trust and respect their boss's approach implicitly, Executive Management will often request a second, outside opinion.

As I've also explained, Strategists usually have no practical, long-term experience in running a business after implementing a plan; ultimately, they haven't had to take ownership of the consequences when a goal doesn't materialize. Practitioners draw from their hands-on history to see a project through to the bitter end, so they can usually tend to any challenges midstream.

Let me stop here and say that I'm *not* trying to pit one against the other. I'm trying to express that the unique contributions of *both* Strategists and Practitioners, if used in combination, can create better results than if the two are not cooperating. I can recall countless conversations I've had with Strategists about projects, and the deeply intellectual and stimulated thought-processes that emerged. A great Strategist is an asset who presses *both* sides to perform at their best, while everyone earns respect.

Different types of people are needed to accomplish any goal. If you were going to try and build a house, having a plan (strategy) would prevent the project from taking ten times longer than it should by rooting out many mistakes before they happened.

A business-related example is an acquisition; it takes a variety of talented Strategists *and* Practitioners to accomplish the task. From scouting opportunities and prospects to negotiating the deal, to planning and implementing a Communication Plan—not one single person has all the skills required, but collectively, a group of Practitioners and Strategists can complete the objective.

This is where you should ask yourself: What is my skill set? Which part of the picture do I provide, and do I know how to interact with others to accomplish the goal? Answering these questions honestly can help you assess yourself and the people you're working with. Then, if you look, you'll find the right/wrong type of Strategist/Practitioner in any particular job position. Let me give you an example of when you know you've found a mismatch of agendas.

One time, I was working on a project, when the company brought in an outside consulting firm that had a reputation for being the world's best strategic partner. The project was focused on historical industry practices, and there weren't too many moving parts. Over the previous four years, we'd hired four other consulting firms, so by this point, we Practitioners had an understanding of ourselves, our future needs, and the corrective changes that were probably needed.

Our business model was intentionally different than others in our industry, which helped us gain an innovative foothold in our market. The consultants we'd previously hired had only recommended that we change our model to be like everyone else's, or they'd just tried to tweak our strategy, but they ended up bringing us nothing new, aside from some low-hanging fruit.

During the latest scoping process with the top strategy firm, I made a request of them. I hoped to prevent these Strategists from making the same mistakes the other consulting firms had made. I said, "Please tell me where the missing links are in our strategy, or give us secrets others have used, so that we can improve ourselves."

Yet again, they either weren't able or weren't willing to do this. The consultants stopped engaging me in interviews and during meetings, and instead, they focused on presenting details to the Senior Executives. They had nothing new to add to our strategy. I knew all the practical pieces of the puzzle, and I could spot weak players right away.

Part of the learning process of being in management involves figuring out what everyone's agenda is. Bosses like to hire outside Strategists for various reasons; sometimes, it's because there is a lack of people in the company who could act as effective Project Managers. Other times, it's because bosses like to orchestrate changes within a company without having to disclose their long-term agendas. Of course, we're all human. Pride, arrogance, greed, or incompetence often factor in to these agendas. Your ability as a manager to recognize these motivators requires experience, and a special awareness. Recognizing hidden agendas can help direct the steps you take, guiding you safely through the minefields to the end of a project. In this case, I had to navigate *very* carefully, as the Strategists were being used to advance ulterior motives from above.

But I also have a story showing some positive dynamics between Practitioners and Strategists. I was working on a difficult acquisition project that took many different strategic meetings to get off the ground. The acquisition was going to consume a lot of limited resources within our company, and it would also have a big impact on the employees and customers of the company we were acquiring. Despite those challenges, we knew that we really needed this acquisition, so my Strategist partner and I developed a plan to transform our business into a stronger, combined model for success.

Selling the idea of the acquisition internally and gaining the resources we needed would be crucial. Knowing this, my partner and I had many conversations to develop a plan for buy-in. Once we presented our ideas, we immediately encountered resistance. I felt sad to see my Strategist partner rebuked and corrected over and over by the support staff. However, in spite of some normal pushback, exchanges with Executive Management were often ego-boosting, when we'd win a point for a moment. Then, we'd be back to countless hours of ego-deflating conversations with the support staff. I got my fair share, but I was going to be there for the long haul, so my opinions weighed more heavily with the group. When the acquisition was complete, I would be running and overseeing the plan far into the future, whereas the Strategist would only be following up with occasional monitoring and would

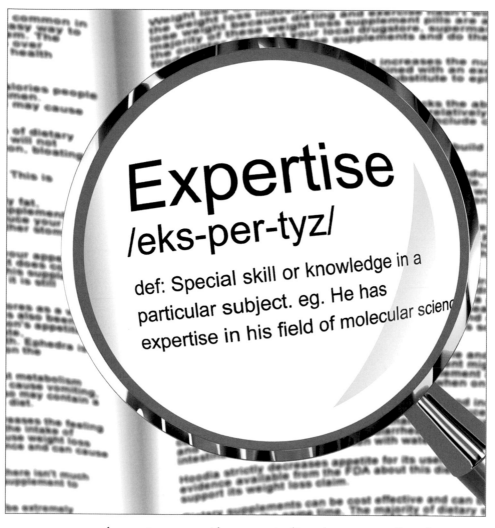

move on to another assignment. Also, practicality plays very well with support staff, and Practitioners (like me) speak directly to that pragmatism.

After much struggling to communicate our strategy, we overcame the resistance, and the acquisition plan moved forward.

What I learned from this particular project is that it can be difficult for anybody, whether a Strategist or a Practitioner, to get approval for a plan. Both types can face rebuke from all different kinds of pushback during the initial phase, just from different angles.

Here are some things to shoot for when you are seeking approval for a new business plan or strategy:

• Have a strong vision of the end result, and communicate with confidence.

• Create the healthy communication lines needed to get buy-in and commitments.

• Access the talent, and determine whether they can perform these changes and operate successfully within the future structure.

• Be aware of your competition/opposition to determine counter moves you might need to make, and so as to not be derailed or out-maneuvered.

• Know your weakness and ask for help; no one knows it all.

• Find a balance between being optimistic and being realistic when you're communicating with everyone.

• Check your ego at the door; remember—people do not like change.

I was very fortunate to have worked under a boss for ten years that recognized my strategic weakness. I joke that in one of my early reviews, my boss gave me a D+ in strategy. The problem was that I was a Practitioner; I was busy getting things done. I couldn't think like a Strategist or even understand the need for strategy. Over the course of my career, I realized that people need to know where you're going with a plan, and especially, what the future will look like. This is where laying out strategies and communicating them effectively pays off, whether managing up or down.

As a kindness, to help me develop this skill-set, my boss gave me numerous assignments in creating and executing strategy. Thank goodness, she also hired internal talent and solid consulting firms to assist while I was learning. Eventually, I acquired their skills by observing their tactical approaches and all the data-mining processes they'd mastered. In today's business world—with Excel, Visio, PowerPoint and so on—we can produce countless reports to slice and dice data, which aids a Strategist in conveying the message. Data can show you history, and if reviewed correctly, it can also show anomalies—areas that need attention. This insight into quantitative information gathering helped me to think and communicate more strategically.

Within a year after my first failing grade in strategy, my boss gave me an A at my next review. The hard work, and the exposure, had given me the boost I needed. I found out that I *hadn't* been deficient at thinking strategically, but that I *had* been deficient at the art of communicating my thoughts. The real learning I experienced was in the arts of crafting Communication Plans, of managing perceptions, and of building the confidence of others.

I also had the great fortune to observe a Master of Strategy for ten years—my boss. She had the unique ability to look into the future while maintaining a strong grasp of the past, with the goal of correcting and learning from all the mistakes and missteps, including her own. She could see the rippling effects of change, whether change had or hadn't happened. There is a cost for inaction, and a benefit to action. It was uncanny listening to her recount stories of incomplete plans or incompetence, or explaining how issues today and in the future could have been resolved if only the right steps had been taken.

Meetings with my boss to discuss strategy and execution were especially brutal for all involved. Being prepared, thinking quickly, and controlling your speech were tools the participants had to learn just to survive. When discussing strategy, the validity of a plan would be tested and countered with questions as to why it was important and when it would deliver its hoped-for results. If you didn't have a solid answer for those two key questions, you set yourself up for further questioning—and she was merciless. If your defensive characteristics arose, or if she sensed weakness, you were a goner.

I remember the way she could identify the people who were simply trying to be the smartest kiss-ass in the room, especially those that regurgitated the comments of others, but tried to own the statement. This is a common tactic to try and get noticed, especially if those running the meeting (or attending it) aren't really paying attention. A common regurgitation is, "Let me put it this way." Or "Let me expand on that." A good listener, or an astute manager, watches everything and can see right through these tactics. My boss would catch them every time. Strategy meetings can have very high stakes and careers can be won or lost with one wrong move.

Before I finish this chapter, let me quickly address the topic of financial matters and how they relate to presenting the numbers with any strategy. I always say, it's all about the money. I've never seen anyone develop a strategic plan that was going to *lose* market shares or cash.

It takes money to make money, and the value of monetary resources plays a huge role in moving forward with any plan. I can remember having to commit to a revenue quote any time there was an internal upgrade, a product enhancement, a product development, an acquisition, or even an uncertain restructuring. If I didn't have business perspective on setting expectations, there is no way I could have committed to new numbers in each of these circumstances.

Over the course of my career, I stayed in tune by becoming friends with the finance people in the company. Numbers talk volumes, and excuses fall on deaf ears. The point is, if you *know* the numbers, you stand a chance of surviving the interrogation that any strategy is going to face. Practitioners and Strategists should both know the flavor of the financials. When it comes to money, new revenue is gold, and if promising this jewel to management, trust me—you will be questioned to death. It's much easier to defend a cost-cutting plan to enhance margins, but creating new revenue is an art. In such a case, the Practitioner has to convince others that they can deliver.

KEYS TO SUCCESS 🗝 *Chapter 4 Review*

- A **Practitioner** is a person who is actively engaged in and qualified for the act or discipline of a certain profession. A **Strategist** is a person who is skilled in formulating and implementing strategy. Typically, Strategists lay out *plans and goals*, while Practitioners *complete objectives*.

- Practitioners can get a bad rap for being limited in their thinking, while Strategists can fall into the trap of lacking **experience** in practical application. Where one lacks *breadth*, the other lacks hands-on *immersion*. Both are important elements of **exposure**.

- Strategists and Practitioners, if used in combination, can create better results than if the two are not cooperating. This will require some maneuvering in **communication**, but a brilliant collaboration can emerge, if successful.

- On any project, no matter which type you are, ask yourself: What *is* my skill set? Which part of the picture do I provide, and do I know how to interact with others to accomplish the goal?

- It takes a lot of experience and a heightened awareness, but try to assess yourself and those around you for special **talents** and **hidden agendas**. Remember you are playing to win; you must sense if you are ahead or behind.

- You should listen well to the tempo and cadence of any meeting; each has its own dynamics.

- When leading an initial strategy session, always be prepared to answer the two toughest questions: "Why?" and "When?". You know they are coming, so be ready. Then, try not to drift into comments or **defensiveness**—stick to the point. If asked to clarify a point, first gain an understanding of which part needs to be clarified.

- Don't worry about gaining the support of your peers or support staff as much as of your bosses; ultimately, *they* make the decisions. All the same, don't alienate your peers or your staff completely; later, you will need *them* aboard.

I will finish here with a thought about taking responsibility when executing any business model. Whatever part you play in the process, Strategist or Practitioner, you *must* own your time, your resources, and your commitment to completing a project. Harness your personal skills, and your ability to engineer miracles through others. I challenge companies to access their most willing talent and to help foster understanding of the differences between *types* of business people. The dynamics of morphing a vision into a reality will challenge everyone to make big changes of their own.

CHAPTER FIVE

The Importance of Communication

Communicating, which is to share or exchange information, sounds simple, but remains one of the most difficult things for human beings to do well. Like it or not, we all have to have conversations. You cannot avoid communicating with others, neither personally nor in business. The purpose of this chapter is to illustrate the importance of fostering an understanding when we communicate—not in order to agree or disagree with each other, but for all to fully comprehend the meaning of what is being said. In other words, I want to get you to *think* more about how you're going to communicate…before you communicate.

Both talking and listening are intertwined in the process of communication. We are not all wired the same way, and the bottom line is that when we're tackling sensitive or biased issues, emotions can override a clear dialogue and create massive misunderstandings. A good example of this is something that happened to me many years ago.

I once went to a couples' retreat with some friends, and at the event, we were all challenged to be better communicators. On the way home—a long drive, with another couple in the back seat—my wife and I started engaging in a conversation, and a word came up that she and I strongly disagreed about. The word was "empathy", and we had different interpretations of its meaning. The couple in the back grew quiet and watched as we discussed, loudly, the semantics of this word, completely abandoning the main topic of our original conversation.

After carrying on this way for several minutes, I said, "Pull up the dictionary, and whatever it says, I'm ok with it. If I'm wrong, I'm wrong!"

Now, if I had been a better student over the weekend event, it would have helped me move away from this word battle, and to steer the conversation back on its intended track. But it was a good lesson, because what I learned was that a single word can have different values or meanings for different people. Using one word incorrectly can spark fireworks. I always love framing this story to friends by saying that I failed couples counseling, but got a great big lesson on the way home in the car.

Another perfect communication anecdote came into being when I was playing cards with some friends one time, husbands against the wives. Each time we changed hands, the team whose turn it was would call the type of game. During the second hand, after the wives had called the game, I noticed that my teammate and I were using very different strategies than the opposing team. We obviously weren't in sync. We'd heard them correctly when they called the game, but each team had taken on a completely different meaning of the rules (if you've ever played H.O.R.S.E, you know it can be difficult to even *remember* the rules), so we were playing entirely different games at the same time. It was so funny when we discovered our mistake that we went the extra step on each hand going forward, pausing to clarify the *actual* rules we were going to play by.

I'll remind you that I retired from the corporate world after a good, long time; I've seen many examples, both personally and at work, of how communication is key in building and maintaining relationships. I've also noticed trends in communication. For instance, in the business realm, emails and texts have overtaken the spoken word. This is somewhat flexible, depending on your age group; but overall, the standard practice in the typical "do-more-with-less-people" corporate structure of today is to email. The same goes for follow-up communications; when things go wrong, the topic tends to be addressed in an email these days, and not always through a direct conversation. The result is that during conference calls, conferences, and the occasional one-on-one meeting, people seem to have lost some of the skills needed to communicate effectively, out loud. Companies are living organizations, and without an effort to speak to one another, there is a diminished return on the company's efforts to succeed.

Communicating up and down in an organization needs to be healthy and routine. In Chapter 2, I outlined how understanding a vision is vital as companies evolve. In Chapter 8, I'll cover how caring for employees creates the environment needed for healthy communication. I cannot stress enough how important it is that people communicate with each other to the best of their abilities.

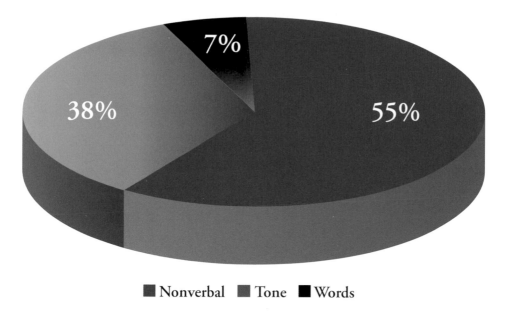

■ Nonverbal ■ Tone ■ Words

Let me illustrate this more fully.

I did a little research on the various forms of communication and found some psychology statistics on the impact and value of certain elements. For instance, in face-to-face communication, the most impactful component is body language (55%), followed by the tone that's being used (38%), and finally, by the actual words being said (7%). When speaking on the phone, the most impactful thing is the tone of voice (87%), and then, the words used (13%). The point is that a lot of communication happens between people on a nonverbal level. It's less about *what* we are saying than it is about *how* we are saying it—our posture, our tone of voice, and our inflections convey emotional messages.

When we communicate via email or text, all of this *real* content is lost. We have words without the accompanying nuances that tell the other person what we are actually trying to say to them. There is a dearth of statistics available on the many mysterious nuances of written communication. It's no wonder that when we are not ear-to-ear, so often there is *mis*communication!

Who's the Boss?

Another thing I've noticed is that the natural pecking order—the hierarchy—in our workplaces can create many barriers to communicating earnestly. How do we speak to our bosses? How do we speak to our peers? Sometimes we may not know our coworkers that well; or maybe, we're dealing with someone we don't fully trust or respect, or who we just don't want to be spending time with. Expressing ourselves politely with people we don't necessarily like takes on unique challenges. But, we should also be careful not to jump to conclusions about how communications must proceed.

Especially when dealing with people who are either lower or higher than us on the ladder, we must be bold. I once had a college psychology professor who had made himself very unpopular by using disparaging classifications for people: making borderline racist comments and expressing sexism (although this was typical in the 70s). At one point, he gave us an IQ test, and I decided to have a little fun with it (these were my passive aggressive days). When it was my turn to take the test, I intentionally got every question wrong, to the best of my ability. When it came time to review my results with the class, the professor announced that I should find a job as a garbage man, or in some other low-intellect job.

So, I grinned and asked, "You didn't even question the fact that your 'A' student has the lowest IQ in the class?"

He looked at me with a huge smile and said, "You got me!"

Here, we broke our way through a hierarchical status quo and found a somewhat earnest exchange. Although passive-aggression towards your superiors won't usually do the trick, it can be necessary (and healthy) to find creative ways to share (and discover) the truth behind people's actions and reactions.

Communicating with bosses is a step up on the challenge scale, and requires a whole new level of skills. First, remember that you're speaking to people who have ambitiously strived to get where they are—that means, like many of us, they have egos. The egos of different bosses vary in degree based on factors like self-awareness, confidence, and insecurity. Learning how to read these personality traits and preparing yourself before you communicate is vital to your being understood. Also, bosses don't like to have their time wasted, so don't carry on too much about the details. Their attention spans may be very short, so have your facts and your answers ready enough so that you can get in and out—fast. Concentrate on expressing overall concepts, clarifying your answers, and getting them to buy in.

I recall a time when I was attending a lot of my boss's staff meetings and watched people approach unprepared and go through hell as a result. One off-the-cuff statement could ruin the day. When communication breaks down in a meeting, focus can be easily lost, and the desire to speak up dwindles, as fewer and fewer people feel like participating. When bosses are to blame for the breakdown, it's the worst. I've witnessed some that are so unconscious of their poor communication styles that they will drive a group crazy in simply trying to get their points across. Senseless rambling, or a preference for conflict, can cause a group of listeners to discount a person's entire message, whether the boss or a staff member is speaking.

Of course, both as a boss and below, I've had my ass handed to me in meetings before on many occasions—but this forced me to *change*. I know that expressing yourself with confidence, but not with your ego, is a platform for strong communication. Anything else can be easily mistaken for weakness. Also, passion—so close to being 'emotional'—can be easily misunderstood in a business setting. You can have passion for people, for the project, or even just a feeling or desire to do a better job. I have this problem in particular.

My passion for a topic and my trust in myself to get the job done sometimes overshadows my communication. I expect *my* bosses to listen and see that things will change in the future according to my vision, but I used to try too hard to sound like I was fluid and open to adjustments. I could tell this was causing me to be misunderstood—I seemed "wishy-washy", one boss told me. My 'coolness' strategy backfired on me so many times that I finally learned that communicating up effectively is mostly about saying—firmly—what they probably want to hear. Letting them figure out how *they* felt about a topic was way more important than what I had to say.

Bosses generally look at all sides of a conversation and question abilities, motives, honesty, and reliability. Any of these qualities, if misunderstood, can cause you to lose the support and respect your boss has for you. So when communicating up, you should remember that many factors are being considered. Confidently demonstrating your thoughtfulness and effectiveness is the goal. After all, that's what they're paying you for!

Innovation in Communication

Even dealing with peers can demand new strategies—and a hell of a lot of patience.

One of the most unpleasant experiences in miscommunication I ever had with a peer was with a woman who led a support team within the bank I worked at. I had never communicated directly with her before. I didn't realize this then, but some bad blood had built up between my group and hers over the years, because she felt we had consistently pushed their help away. My group was very independent and experienced, and many times, we just hadn't felt we needed it. She was naturally competitive, so this had ruffled her feathers.

I had just been promoted and I knew that our future interactions would increase, so as I was passing by her office, I knocked on the door and said, "Can we have a few minutes, or should I come back later? I just wanted to say hello." I wanted to open up the dialogue about working together.

She immediately waved me in and I sat down in the chair across from her at her desk. She didn't wait a second before saying, "Your persona precedes you. I will not be your doormat. If you fucking screw with me, I will take you down."

Ok. I sat back in the chair as if she'd punched me in the gut. I took a big breath and said, in a low, calm voice, "This is not an acceptable way of communicating with me under any circumstances. If you have a problem with me without knowing anything about me, then you're heading towards your own demise."

I got up and walked back to my office. Later, I discussed our encounter with her boss, and I basically said I thought she wasn't good for the organization. If she couldn't get along with me, for no apparent reason, then this wasn't going to work. Two days later, she came into my office. Before I knew it, she had closed the door, and she took a seat across from me at my desk.

"I'm sorry for my comments and the harshness I expressed towards you the other day," she said.

I asked her if there was anything I could do to help her communicate better in the future. If she wanted to change, then I would be happy to mentor her. She told me she'd been advised before about her short temper. From that moment on, we agreed that whenever she felt like she was going to lose her temper, she was to look at me and remember this talk. (It had to be nothing more than a distraction to help her let the moment pass and not blow up.) Without a doubt, we all have to deal with incompetent and irritating people at work, which can stretch our patience and politeness to the breaking point. But blowing up was not productive. She understood this now, and we got along much better after that.

When Communication Fails

Unfortunately, communication can sometimes malfunction from above, from below, and at every point in between.

Late in my career, I was faced with the task of communicating to my boss some changes to the original plan for a major project. This wasn't due to any mistakes, but simply, to a lack of complete information at the time of planning. It was time to give my boss an update from my group, which meant I needed to communicate all the diversions from the plan that had been made since our last meeting. My boss didn't like surprises, and I knew deep down that I should have communicated in between these updates to get each change approved, one by one. It was common sense, but I had ignored it, and now, I had a feeling I would be scolded.

As expected, once I introduced the changes (that were already in motion), my boss informed me that I had lost credibility in his eyes. In reality, I had improved our outcome and demonstrated creativity in my solution-based performance, but because I had ineffectively communicated, the changes were thrown out. My boss *could* have just thanked us for thinking on our feet, and then taken credit for the success of the project later on, and we wouldn't have minded—but unfortunately, that didn't happen, either.

KEYS TO SUCCESS 🔑 *Chapter 5 Review*

- **Communicating**, which is to share or exchange information, sounds simple, but is actually quite complex. Both talking—and listening—are involved. A single word can have different values or meanings for different people, and using just one word incorrectly can spark disagreement.

- Both personally and professionally, communication is key in building and maintaining **relationships**. In the modern corporate world, because of a "do-more-with-less-people" mentality, emails and texts have overtaken the spoken word. The result is that, in person, people have lost some of the skills needed to communicate effectively.

- *Body language and tone* are more impactful elements of communication than the actual words we use. Thus, **written communication** seems to be even *more* complicated for us to interpret cleanly. If we're not extremely careful, this can be a catalyst for grave *mis*communication!

- Communicating up, down, and across a perceived **hierarchy** can also have its challenges. But we must be *bold and innovative* in discovering new truths behind people's *actions and reactions*.

- Communicating with bosses requires dealing with **egos**, and learning how to gage their levels of confidence, self-awareness, and insecurity. Rather than getting caught up in details, concentrate on expressing overall concepts, clarifying your answers, and getting them to buy in. For your own part, try to demonstrate your *thoughtfulness and effectiveness* with confidence, but *not* with your ego.

KEYS TO SUCCESS   🔑   *Chapter 5 Review (continued)*

- In business situations, be wary of communicating with **passion**—which can seem overly 'emotional'—and, equally, of speaking too 'coolly'—which can seem wishy-washy. Just don't try too hard, either way! You have to learn to toe the line with bosses, who are constantly evaluating *your* abilities, motives, honesty, and reliability. Instead of worrying about what *you* have to say, the best strategy is to say—firmly—what they probably want to hear, while letting them figure out exactly what that is.

- Dealing with peers can be surprisingly taxing, especially when we do not really know—or *like*—our coworkers. *Trust and respect* are difficult to muster in these situations, and they are fundamental to positive communication. We all have to deal with incompetent and irritating people at work, which can stretch our patience and politeness to their breaking points. Remember, above all, that **blowing up is not productive.**

- If you fail to communicate in a timely manner with a boss, you can destroy the **credibility** of even your best work. Never set changes in motion without communicating up. Even if you're thinking well on your feet and protecting the goals of everyone involved, your boss could throw all of your hard work into the trash simply because the integrity of the communication was compromised.

We need to communicate with others with an increased awareness of the dynamics at play. More importantly, organizations need to inquire about the communications happening within to determine their overall health. Without effective communication as a standard practice, it is difficult to recover revenue and talent once they are lost. I hope that I've shed some light on many of the situations in which good communication is vital, both in your business and in your life.

CHAPTER SIX

You Sell Daily

I seldom hear people say that they *like* to "sell". The first thing that comes to mind when we think of selling is a used-car salesman type of person; we equate "selling" with "structured sales" or "hard sales"—and awkward situations. Feeling uncomfortable with selling isn't uncommon, but we *do* sell every day of our lives, and we don't even know it! Let me explain.

Selling is really about adding value. Ask yourself: Do I add value in my conversations with others? If you do, then you are selling. It could be your point of view that you're selling, or a worthy game plan, or a valuable lesson. *Teaching* or *persuading* others by giving them access to your perspective is the only way we can hope to improve anyone—including ourselves.

Let's go back to our feared example of the used-car salesperson. Yes, his is a formulated and successful approach to selling, like it or not. These men and women are in business to sell you a big-ticket item, but at the core, they are actually just talking you into purchasing something…of some value. I've been in Retail and Commercial Sales my entire career and I've experienced many types of sales with many different inherent dynamics, but one thing is constant: Any time you are selling yourself or a company's products or services, you present a *value proposition*. This is, literally, how you *propose* to add value.

When I worked at Sears in the late 70s, it was understood that Craftsman tools and Sears-brand appliances were the best in the market. We carried superior products in these areas, and our customer base knew it, so selling in these departments was like taking candy from a baby. Not all of the departments worked like this, though; for instance, Sporting Goods and Shoes were much harder to sell. In *those* departments, it took skill to persuade people to buy products of a quality equal to that of our competitors' items.

In the Shoe Department, we all sold for commissions, which made it aggressive and competitive. It wasn't uncommon to hear the salespeople making statements that made the customers feel good about themselves in order to get them to buy more shoes. There, it was all about emotions and self-esteem. Alternatively, selling in the Sporting Goods or Hardware Departments was all about being macho; having a tough physical appearance or an outdoorsy, do-it-yourself attitude would help persuade customers to get on board. But the selling task was not simple in any of these areas.

One year, after the Christmas sales season, I got placed in the Women's Clothing Department to handle returns. The department was currently only staffed for normal sales volumes, and it would need extra help fielding the inevitable flood of returned gift items that came in after the holidays.

But in just a day of work here, I began noticing something peculiar. To my surprise, women's undergarments were among the items most frequently returned. Even stranger, each time, I had to ask the customer several questions, since a handwritten form was required for every one (remember, this was the 70s). When I got to the part where I had to ask the women for the reason why they were returning the item, many of them actually blushed before answering. Since the inquiry was coming to them from a young man, they often had to answer—uncomfortably—on the fly. The subject was so sensitive that I quickly learned to speak directly while keeping my head down at the same time, just to get the form filled out and the whole thing over with. Most of the women cleverly answered that the style or color of the undergarment wasn't to their liking, when we both knew it was actually the fit that was the problem.

This is where selling came into play, in the opposite of the expected direction: These *women* felt they had to sell me on the reason they were returning their items. I didn't actually care why they were returning them, and the store didn't really care, either, but for some reason, the women thought it mattered. This is a good example of how, even as apparent customers, we *sell* on a daily basis—often, we find ourselves convincing others of our motives or purpose.

When it comes to being sold, however, most of us are usually skeptics. Trust does not come easily, and a salesperson's communication skills play a huge role in whether or not we decide to buy their reasoning, and in the traditional scenario, their item. In every case, they are selling more than just a product; they are selling facts, concepts, and even beliefs. Our perceptions are made up of many complex thoughts and emotional experiences, and changing a customer's perception can be impossible, at times, for even the most skilled salesperson.

Every time we meet with people, either one-on-one or in a small group, there is an opportunity to build a relationship and to develop trust. The in-person environment allows for a level of interaction that cannot be accomplished in texts, emails, letters, or even phone calls. Most likely, in spite of our techie age, you sell in person at this level every day at the office, at social events, and even at home. You might not think that you're selling, but you are.

Early in my banking career, I was placed in the new Accounts Department for training, with only one other person. Our points of contact with existing and prospective customers were important to the bank, so they were supposed to be made during sit-down meetings. I was transitioning from the Sears-style stand-up floor approach to the one-on-one sit-down environment, and what

I learned was that facing the customer in an intimate setting allowed us both to engage in a deeper and more exploratory conversation. This opened the door for showing customers that we really cared about their needs and valued their time.

Later on in my banking career, and as I progressed as a salesperson, my interactions with the vendors at conventions became just as important as my meetings with prospects. It's a small world, and we all sold to the same banks. Vendors' profits are more commission-based than bankers', which makes them more cutthroat. At these conventions, if vendors liked you, they would make sure your deals went smoothly, but if they didn't—they'd make your life a living hell.

To grease the wheels, I often attended vendor dinners, where there would be heavy drinking to help get a friendly exchange going between us. One night during a convention, I joined a bunch of vendors for drinks even after dinner. The cocktails and shots were flowing, and we were discussing sales techniques and bantering pleasantly. At one point, I brought up the word "persuasion", using it to describe a style of conversation within the sales cycle.

Unbeknownst to me, there was a young woman—a software vendor—sitting at the table next to us, eavesdropping on our conversation. She'd overheard what I'd said, and she immediately pulled up a chair to our table and sat down. She made sure she was facing me directly.

"I disagree," she said. I looked at her curiously. Not one to back down from a challenge, I decided to engage. I asked her name; it was Sunny Williams.

"I was saying, Sunny, that a form of conversation to get a prospect to agree with you is called 'persuasion'," I repeated. "What don't you agree with?"

"I don't agree with the word 'persuasion'," Sunny said.

"Well, then what would you call it?" I asked.

Sunny didn't lose a moment. "If 'persuasion' is being used, that implies that you're lying, and taking advantage of them."

I looked around at the table for help. The rest of the group was watching with interest, but politely staying out of it. This woman was so inflamed, that nobody wanted in. They figured I could handle the heat.

Sunny had lots more to say about the subject of persuasion, and I let her finish.

Then I asked her if when she's talking to a person, she has the need to be understood. She paused for a second to comprehend what I was asking.

"Yes," she said.

"So what word would you use to describe it when you're attempting to get someone else to understand what you're saying?" I pressed her.

She paused again.

"Well, it would have to be a word that didn't resemble…manipulation," she said.

I could see where this was going. The real implication here was that I manipulated people.

"I would use a word like 'openness' or 'transparency' to describe my communicating with someone I wanted to understand me," Sunny continued.

Now, this was mostly just another argument over semantics. There was no real winner or loser to be made here. So I let the conversation die out, and once the entertainment value of the argument had diminished, the group returned to its congenial bantering. But it occurred to me later that Sunny had been sitting by herself before she came over, watching a big table of people B.S.ing and having fun. She probably felt left out, and was looking for an entrance into the nest. And what better entry was there than to challenge the head of the conversation by trying to *sell* him on an alternate perspective?

How many times a day do you speak your mind? This is the art of *persuading* your audience to see your view and value your opinions. Like it or not, this is selling yourself. Some are blessed with the skills and abilities to pull this off with ease, and others create a lot of agony by arguing to try and prove a point.

Many years after that, though I was still in the Sales Department, I was asked to temporarily oversee the Product Management Department while its permanent Manager was overseas on a travel assignment. My boss had managed this department himself years ago and felt it would be a good experience for me. Since it was a short-term placement, I saw it as a chance to learn more about the functionality and processes of Product Management, as well as to gain a better understanding of the people who supported my own department's efforts. I joked that since I was always complaining about this department's slowness in turning out better products, it must be my punishment to be assigned a managerial role here.

Soon, I knew that Product Managers presented new concepts for roll out during a routine meeting, wherein they had to get approval from at least six Department Heads. They had to sell their ideas to the group, over and over. There were always IT resource limitations, money obstacles, and interdependency challenges that Product Managers had to overcome in order to get their projects approved. Sitting in on the meetings showed me that there were a lot of internal sales going on at our bank, and they were just as vital as the outside sales going on through my own department.

At the first routine Product Management meeting I attended, I quickly caught on to which of the managers had good or bad selling skills. Not all of them were well-equipped. Even though some of them were clearly brilliant, their presentations missed the mark, and being unable to close the deal meant a lost revenue opportunity for the company.

In what little time I had to get my hands dirty, I decided to have a staff meeting with all of the Product Managers to recap my observations from the meeting. I was direct and to the point; I told them that I now understood they were as important as my sales staff and that selling better internally would help them advance their projects. I pointed out examples of two of the managers who were clearly skilled at selling and whose effortless presentations had flown them through the meeting with approval. Then, I pointed out two product managers who had been plagued with setbacks from the Department Heads. The irony was that the two who had gotten "yeses" were requesting much more difficult things of Upper Management than the ones who had gotten "nos".

The real difference was that the approved managers had crafted their messages to *win* the sales game. They showed confidence in their knowledge of the products *and* in their mastery of people skills, and they had already developed trusted relationships with the Department Heads. The stage was set for their grand performances, and they pulled them off with aplomb.

I knew that on the whole, the Product Managers had a long way to go, but in my brief stint as their manager, I planted the seeds for improvement. Later on, I became one of the Department Heads to whom they had to present their ideas, and I was happy to see that they tried much harder to sell in the way that I had prescribed.

KEYS TO SUCCESS 🗝 *Chapter 6 Review*

- **Selling** is about adding—or justifying—*value*. We do this every day by *teaching* or *persuading* others of our perspectives.

- Are you worrying about how you might be perceived? Use **communication skills** to sell, and be yourself; people want to know whom they are really dealing with, and first impressions matter. Don't be an actor, parroting lines from a course or lesson manual on selling—it'll show.

- As with any good communication, **listen** more and talk with fewer words. Tone of voice and body language speak volumes.

- Always **be direct** with your responses to objections. You can have go-to statements as long as you don't parrot them. Do your pre-work, as an unprepared moment on the spot can cause instability in the sale.

- Be aware of the **interdependencies** in your business. Does your team have the resources and capabilities to deliver on the promises you're making? Overcoming pushback is a process, not an insurmountable hurdle, so turn this into steps toward success.

- Who are you selling for? Are you pushing your needs (or the company's needs) down the customer's throat? Or are you trying to benefit everybody involved? You need to have a winner's mentality, but be careful of being too **cutthroat**. Remember that even when commissions are involved, the art of persuasion is more about appealing to your crowd and having a *transparent* discussion.

- One-on-one, **in-person meetings** are best for developing <u>trust</u> in the long-term relationships you are cementing as a salesperson. Since we're *all* skeptical of being sold, stay attentive to the pacing and the timing needed to close a deal, and remember to have *patience*.

I cannot stress more how important it is to work on being a better salesperson. We sell ourselves daily, and we should aim not just to get people buy into our concepts and agree with our opinions, but also, to foster a better understanding as to where we all are coming from. I challenge everyone, in any type of job or industry, to develop an awareness of and a skill set in the sales we do wherever we go.

PART THREE

Mentorship

Let Mentorship Be Your Guide

CHAPTER SEVEN

The Value of Mentorship

Mentorship is simple to understand, but it is not always as easy to provide or to receive. In a **mentor-mentee relationship**, both participants must be willing to make the time, and to make changes as they learn. As I mentioned in Chapter 3, I have experienced mentorship in many forms throughout my career, even from micromanagers. Mentorship is a necessity for bettering ourselves, and it's not a one-way process; both the mentor and the mentee receive many insights, and in the long run, both gain the pride of having grown significantly through a shared experience.

These days, as a retired corporate manager, I still frequently mentor others. I often say if people want my care, advice, and guidance—it's free. If they don't want help, they are on their own. It takes the *decision* to change, and to allow others to help you, to become successful. I know this because I resisted the help of others for many years, and this resistance was a lingering pitfall throughout my career. As we learned in Chapter 4, just because you *know* something doesn't always mean you know how to *practice* it, and sadly, I didn't understand this irony for a long time.

My earliest experience of being mentored was by my swim coach in high school. Up until that time, I was just a defiant, lost, free spirit—"damaged goods", as they call it today. I really needed to know that someone cared for me without needing anything back. I had little to give at this time, besides my commitment to swimming. My coach had sons younger than me, so I guess that teaching me skills for competition, encouraging me, and caring for me came naturally to him. His instructions were simple: put in the time and effort, and the results will happen. There wasn't too much instruction on the mental aspects of being an athlete, but with his help, I still excelled. By the end of high school, under his tutelage, I had slid easily into a leadership position on our swim team. He had me arrange the next year's season with the other schools and started urging me to become a coach, too. He saw more in me than I did in myself. That's the way it is in most cases of mentorship.

In Chapter 3, I also mentioned my second strong mentor, Mr. Jenkins. Just as influential as my swim coach, Mr. Jenkins showed me the ropes of managing a department at Sears and made sure I caught the attention of Upper Management for my leadership skills. Before we go much further, though, let me point out that a mentor doesn't *need* to be your boss, but simply, someone with the heart to care and the wisdom to provide guidance. You never know where mentorship will come from, so keep your eyes open for every possible opportunity.

In my 36-year-long banking career, there were many other mentors along the way. I remember a boss by the name of Mrs. Ferguson, a strong and stoic woman in an Upper Management position, who had earned respect for running the largest and most visible branch at an otherwise all-male manager bank. She never dressed or acted 'like a man'—she was all woman, and proud of it. This was the late 70s, and she had broken through quite a ceiling. When it came to mentoring me, she said I was a "piece of cake".

I remember asking Mrs. Ferguson a question one time that I probably already should have known the answer to, and she pointed at the Operational Policies Manual on the shelf. "Did you read up on the topic?"

Of course, I hadn't. At that moment, I made it a point to memorize the Operational Policies, instead of burdening her with simple questions going forward. The next time, I asked her questions about things that were less accessible. She noticed this change in me, so she took more time to explain which of the things I was asking about were most important. She was a very direct woman, and she always made sure I understood what she was telling me. Once again, the mentorship was a success due both to *my* willingness to learn and change, and to *her* willingness to take the time to provide me with what I needed.

When I elevated to a management position at that bank, what skills I had were stretched to their limit, because I was still so young. Only by making lots of mistakes did I gain the **self-awareness** necessary to be a better manager and person. (We'll talk more about self-awareness in Chapters 8 and 12.) A couple of years after that, I started to be seen as adept at "Crisis Management", and the higher-ups began sending me into problem offices for short-term damage control. They also asked me to develop long-term strategies to prevent future problems. I think the fact that I was young actually helped; they saw that I was energetic, but also, adaptable.

I accumulated a lot of experience during this time, and I *became* a people person. I learned it's all about the people, and nothing more. Mentoring people in a crisis situation is difficult mainly because time is especially of the essence. Identifying *which* people have the true desire to improve their situations and making time to mentor *them* is extremely important. If the appropriate employees in a bank are not mentored and led, all hell will break loose, eventually.

Later on in my career, I learned that finding the appropriate mentor is just as important. A good mentor will want to impart wisdom and advance good causes; a bad mentor may want to offer guidance, but he or she will use it as a way to manipulate or control you. A self-centered mentor might show you the right way, but only by example of what *not* to do—such as restricting freedoms, or engendering mistrust or fear. A good mentor, on the other hand, will give you and others the freedom to express concerns or give suggestions, while allowing all mentees to feel important and included.

Come from Caring

While developing my own management style, I attended many courses, and one of these stands out in my mind as particularly relevant to the mentorship topic. The premise of the course, as we discussed in Chapter 5, was that listening was more important than trying to convince someone to buy your product or idea. The same can be said about mentoring; listening is more important than convincing. If you want someone to value your opinions and suggestions, they need to know, first and foremost, that you hear them.

For instance, when I moved up to a Senior Management position in the bank, I needed to assess my staff's performance and their capabilities going forward. So, no matter what their age or experience level, I would ask them, "What do you want to be when you grow up?" and I would listen thoughtfully to their answers. The question always got a pause, and then opened up a conversation about past events and future dreams. This created a flow of information in which I could offer guidance, suggestions, or more thought-provoking questions. It is my belief that most people go through their entire careers without working towards something they love and have a passion for. Passion drives purposeful goal-setting, and providing an ear as a mentor is a great way to put others on a path toward their most fulfilling visions in the workplace.

One time, I mentored one of my staff who was in her late 20s, and it had a major impact on us both. This woman was intelligent, driven, creative, and forward thinking, and because her generation grew up in a very different time than mine, her perspective was an absolute asset to our work together. My interactions with her taught me so much; she changed the way I thought about certain issues, and yet, she remained open to my suggestions. The world does evolve, and a mentor needs to realize that in order to continue growing, some concepts and perceptions will need to evolve as well.

This brings me to another tricky facet of mentoring. When a male manager undertakes a female mentee, there is a specific set of challenges to face. Professionalism and honesty become paramount, as the vulnerability of the conversations and their time together can easily make way for a suspicious—or risky—environment. The first way I have found to avoid any issues of impurity is to have mentorship meetings at breakfast or lunch in open, public areas—not in the office, and not at later hours. The second way is to keep yourself in check that you genuinely care about helping the person, making sure there is no need for power, validation, or other gratification at play.

I have found that a man being mentored by a woman—as I have been in several cases—is just as sensitive. HR is equally aware of the potential issues between heterosexual males and females and tends to be cautious about these mentorships. But I strongly believe that if one gender cannot receive the wisdom and guidance of the other, we will continue to have major problems with equality and opportunity in the workplace.

Since these pairings are valuable, we must simply be conscious. Watch out for the jealousy that can be created by mentoring the opposite sex. Your partner,

or the partner of the person being mentored, could easily misunderstand or mistrust the relationship. It is imperative that the partners of both people involved are included in the mentorship process—not only to prevent jealousy, but also, because they need to be on board with the changes their loved ones will go through. This allows partners to be supportive of the transformation, rather than being caught off guard.

Another sensitive topic is mentorship of people who belong to an ethnic minority. As I mentioned in Chapter 3, I spent my childhood attending schools with mostly black and Hispanic students. This spared me from developing racial prejudices, but unfortunately, I have noticed that these exist in many of my colleagues, even today. I recall a period where my bank was attempting to bring awareness to discrimination in the workplace. The Executives hired two women from Northern California to lead regional classes, and they asked managers from all parts of the bank to attend. For many of us, it was the first chance we'd had to meet the other managers. Since I participate with vigor and openness at every opportunity, I was pretty vocal during these meetings, and this won the support of my instructors. At the end of one of the classes, they asked me if I had anything to add, and I asserted: "If we just truly cared for all of our employees, we wouldn't need to be here right now." Though my comment was risky, the instructors agreed, and thanked me. Obviously, I didn't become very popular among the other managers, but that didn't matter to me.

Have a Ball

Mentorship allows great people to gravitate towards other great people, for the benefit of all. When we neglect to help others, it causes a rippling effect throughout an organization. When we work to incorporate mentorship into institutional leadership, instead, we fulfill an ongoing mission, giving those under us a chance to then mentor others. The adage that we are only as strong as our weakest link also applies here. If we don't invest the time and effort in guiding and sharing wisdom with others, how can we build the strength of our work force?

There is one enduring mentorship relationship I have had for over ten years. It was formed in a highly unusual way, under almost negative circumstances, but it later became a working partnership, and wonderful friendship, as well.

Jorge and I had been working at the same bank for several years, and he sat in the cubicle next to mine, although we worked for different departments and hardly ever saw each other. The way our spaces were arranged, I never had to walk past Jorge's desk to get to my own. The only time I ever needed to pass by him was for meetings, to file expense reports, or to put away my paperwork. The rest of the time, I was out on sales calls.

It was years into our non-relationship when Jorge and I found ourselves applying for the same management position, in *his* department. He was already a Relationship Manager there, so it was a big upset when he learned that *I* had gotten the job. He felt slighted, and it put our new working relationship under immediate strain.

When I took the position, I was given background information on all the people in the department, but this was really just a collection of facts on paper. The attitudes of staff members towards one another were more important, and I'd picked up on a large degree of fighting and negative comments— residue from the management vacancy, and from the previous manager. So, after a few brief meetings with each employee one-on-one, including Jorge, I called together a larger staff meeting to discuss what would be my new management approach.

I held the meeting in a small conference room and first, I talked through my background and explained my role in the department. Then, I let everyone speak. They all aired out their grievances. At the end of the meeting, I asked them to work out the animosity among them, and to heal their relationships. I told them that if they acted like adults, I would treat them like adults, but if they continued to act like children, I would have to treat them as such. It was their choice. This caught everyone off guard—but to *my* surprise, by the time we had our next staff meeting, they'd actually worked it all out.

Jorge and I didn't yet know each other very well, but I knew that he was in the midst of bringing in a very large prospect for our bank. The deal was complex, and there were both financial pressures and internal politics at work to get the client on board faster. I asked to meet with Jorge to discuss the game plan. I made every effort to make sure he knew I was interested in his success. This was the first time I offered mentorship to Jorge, and he didn't resist; he was thankful.

Jorge was able to bring the client on board in full accordance with the bank's requirements, and he then decided to attend a convention in Orlando that was relevant to his new customer's industry segment. *I* decided to invite myself along, and when I told Jorge, he was shocked—in a good way. He even changed hotels to accompany me when I arrived, since all the hotels near the convention were already sold out.

The second day of the convention, there were no planned meetings, so Jorge and I agreed to meet at the hotel pool bar to have a beer and to talk. One beer turned into twelve (it was two-for-one!), and our conversation began flowing freely and honestly. Our friendship grew fast, and the lingering misunderstandings between us cleared fully by the time we got up from our barstools to wobble back to our rooms. We walked along close to the edge of the pool, laughing and joking, on our way to wash up before our individual dinner plans. I waited for a safe opportunity to strike, and when he wasn't paying attention, I pushed him into the water.

For a second, Jorge just floundered there, sputtering for air, looking up at me, dumbfounded.

"Stand up!" I said. "It's only 5 feet deep!"

I jumped in to join him, laughing, and Jorge got into it, too. We took turns going down the water slide and taking laps around the neighboring river run in our inner tubes. By the end of it, we looked like two drowned rats, still in our shirts and shorts; but we had cemented an incredible friendship.

I'm sure if HR had found out about our playful moment, we'd have been in big trouble—but that never happened. To this day, Jorge tells the story about how I tried to drown him on a trip, and that it bonded us for life.

I had plans for Jorge that would unfold over the next ten years. I wanted him to look for more management roles in his future, and he asked me to help him prepare more as a mentor than as a boss. I felt honored, and I dedicated time and energy to it. By the last year before I left that job, Jorge was a thriving manager. Now, he's confident enough to challenge me when he thinks I'm wrong, humble enough to admit when he's made a mistake, and passionate enough to persist. These valuable qualities are the result of good mentorship.

KEYS TO SUCCESS 🔑 *Chapter 7 Review*

- Mentorship is simple to understand, but it is not always as easy to provide or to receive. It's not a one-way street, and in a **mentor-mentee relationship**, both participants must be willing to *make the time*, and to *make changes* as they learn and grow.

- A mentor doesn't need to be your boss, but simply, someone with the *heart to care* and the *wisdom to provide guidance*. A mentee, on the other hand, needs to do his/her part and become familiar with any basics necessary to excel in his/her role. Just because you *know* something doesn't always mean you know how to *practice* it, and a mentor will improve your practice only if you first **decide** to learn all you need to know. When choosing to mentor others, you must focus on those who are **committed** to change, not on those who will waste your time.

- Equally, there are good mentors and bad mentors. Good mentors can listen and are **self-aware**. Bad mentors **manipulate** in order to forward their own agendas, and are self-centered. Both may want to be your guide, so choose wisely.

- **Prejudices** and other difficulties exist in different dynamics between mentor and mentee. *Gender and ethnic differences* can be a challenge, and we should be as sensitive as possible to the feelings of both our mentees and their loved ones. Still, if we come from a place of **truly caring**, none of the differences will really matter.

- Remember that mentors *can* be peers, not only outright superiors. So don't forget to **have a ball!** True and lasting friendships can grow from the *loyalty and fun* fostered by great mentor-mentee relationships.

- We can see the **value** of our own roles as mentors in the eventual *confidence, humility, and passion* of our mentees. Someone who has benefited from your service will be unafraid of challenging you, but equally open to feedback and to admitting his/her own flaws, because he/she will have the passion to *continue* learning and growing.

I hope this chapter has motivated you to learn all that you can about the benefits of being a mentor, or of being mentored. There are immense numbers of articles, books, and classes on this topic, so there's no excuse for not finding ways to incorporate strong and healthy mentorship programs into your business.

CHAPTER EIGHT

Why Counseling is Vital

Really, who likes getting reprimanded when things go wrong?

Even the mildest correction from a boss or other superior can switch us into self-preservation mode. It's normal to feel under attack—even our posture changes, and we immediately spring to our own defense. But in the corporate world, you *can* avoid having to face the issues behind the scolding. Some of us are adept at sidestepping unnecessary conflict, while others of us are really in denial about our flaws, dismissing any and all confrontation with a simple, "What are you talking about?"

In business, events happen—good and bad—that create opportunities to correct and to counsel employees. These conversations should focus on the behavioral changes needed to improve the performance of the person, and of the organization. If we skip our fundamental counseling task, our employees will have no knowledge of management's expectations, making *their* task of not letting the bosses down impossible. By giving an employee a road map to follow—complete with any warning signs—he or she will have a better chance of staying out of the ditches.

As employees, knowing how to adjust and recover from our mistakes can give us a wider perspective, and there's great value in this for the long-term, both personally and professionally. (If you weren't reprimanded occasionally in childhood, you could not possibly function in adulthood.) Life teaches us that time and again, we'll get corrected: in the sports we play and in our jobs; by our teachers, and even by our spouses.

I am *not* a psychologist or a professional counselor—I am just a retired corporate manager who has benefited from various forms of criticism and counseling over the 36-year span of my banking career. Part of growing up in any career is learning to acknowledge that mistakes *do* happen. We are not perfect. (Anyone who says, "I am!" can stop reading this book now.) I recall countless times when I have been counseled, and today, I know those times were blessings, even though back then, they were very emotional and stressful experiences.

I can remember once, when I was the new Operations Officer for a certain branch, I executed a demand from the government to close and forward a customer's funds before checking to see if the customer had taken out a loan to try and replenish it. I was already working at another branch by the time the issue was brought to my attention. As it turns out, one of my mentors had made a loan to this customer, and the mistake I'd made had put in jeopardy the customer's ability to pay it off. My mentor had to do *his* duty and report my error to Upper Management. I remember it felt personal to me at the time; it made me angry. It had to have been hard on my mentor, too, but it had to be done.

My direct manager dealt with me correctly, and when I was done being counseled, I fully understood the magnitude of the situation I'd created in my haste. As a result, I thought more broadly in the future about my actions and how they might affect others, even when I was under the gun.

Another time, I was interviewing for a job with a former employer; he knew my weaknesses well, and he took the opportunity to counsel me on them. He specifically cited my management style and said that I got too close to my employees, and also, that sometimes my social life tended to overshadow my job. All of this was true. He said if I made the appropriate changes, he would give me a chance with his company. Because he wasn't afraid to be brutally honest with me, when I got the position, I did the best job I have ever done. Later in my career, I hired *him* when I was in a crisis at another bank. This was when I'd been appointed the Acting President of the Thrift and Loan that was in trouble with the FDIC; he came on as my Chief Credit Administrator and saved my butt. Because of our previous mentor-mentee relationship, I trusted him, and he trusted me.

Constructive criticism can have a beneficial effect on relationships, but the responsibility is not to be taken lightly. For counseling to be effective, *self-awareness* needs to be present on both sides; both parties need to be prepared, and the wellbeing of the person being counseled has to be taken heavily into account.

I can think of a specific example of a time when a counseling session failed because the counselor took the situation too lightly. This new manager at the company I was working at was given the task of reducing staff in some of our departments—not based on performance, but for other strategic reasons. Still, the manager made up a list of names based on recent numbers alone, and then, he started firing accordingly. At one point, he called an exit-counseling session to let go of an employee who had been with the company for many years. During the session, the manager told him in a very nonchalant way that they were eliminating his job. The meeting went sour, fast. The employee asked the manager if he knew anything about his career or his past performance. He didn't. The manager hadn't done any real preparation; all he had was some math on a page. The manager backpedaled, but the damage was already done. The counseling session ended on a negative note, and HR took witness.

Clearly, a large number of lawsuits are generated as a result of management not addressing serious issues appropriately, and of the biases that some managers have. In so many situations, these cases are dealt with out of court to protect a company's reputation. I have always said that telling the truth and doing what is right is in your best interest. (Sometimes, though, a lawsuit can't be prevented, even if management is nothing but professional and courteous during exit counseling.)

Another important factor in counseling is a prompt response time. Dog trainers will often tell you that your pet will quickly forget what it's done wrong, and if you try to correct it too late, it won't know why it is being punished. The result is that the pet comes away with a misunderstanding and an all-too-general 'bad feeling' about its experience. Humans aren't much different, although thankfully, we do remember events, and we usually know when we've done something wrong—most of the time, even while we are doing it. But if the issue is avoided and not confronted immediately, the result will still be uncertainty, the breakdown of communication, and a weakened future productivity.

My early managerial roles required me to counsel many employees, since I was a sort of "clean up artist" within the bank. I do have a soft heart towards people, and this made my many interactions difficult at times, but I believe it also made me all the more suited for my job. I think that an honest mistake can always be corrected, but that a dishonest mistake cannot. Sorting out the truth is crucial, including figuring out the cause of any error. Sometimes naïve or neglectful actions can cause a mistake to happen, while other times, there is a clear act of intentional dishonesty. Sometimes, it's even easier to counsel a corrupt person who doesn't really care, because the case is just so simple to judge. For instance, I remember being sent to Sacramento to oversee a teller who was balancing an ATM, with the aim of figuring out who was at fault for what *seemed* like stealing: him or the machine. We had no security cameras back then, and the ATM was kicking out an extra $40 to $60 each week that was not being accounted for. After only two days, I determined that he was pocketing the money. Our counseling session was immediate and quick; I fired him.

But often, it's difficult to understand a situation, and the motives behind even a shifty mistake. The person who erred doesn't usually need to be hanged—just corrected. I remember a salesperson who got caught red-handed lying to a manager about his whereabouts. This employee was a man who had been in our Operations Center working for 10 or 15 years and, I suspect, he was never promoted because of his race. His boss, a real stickler, gave him a warning that if he lied again, he would be terminated. After his reprimand, he was contrite; he was genuinely ashamed he'd let us down. He admitted that he had been completely overwhelmed by the pressure piled up against him. People make mistakes, and you can't throw *everyone* out. After his 90-day probation, he'd again proven to us that he could handle his job. He turned out to be committed to improving his sales skills in order to meet our expectations.

Helping a person who really cares about his/her job—and who sincerely wants to change—through a difficult situation can be rewarding. This doesn't mean that mistakes don't have to be cleaned up; it just means that trust and dependability can be rebuilt. It's the job of the person being counseled to improve, and the job of the person counseling to acknowledge the person's change.

So, what about *bad* counseling? The temperament, perspectives, and expectations of the counselor play a big role in how guidance and criticism are received. An aggressive micromanager (as we saw in Chapter 3) can turn a counseling session into a volatile confrontation that is uncomfortable for all involved. If the boss doesn't already have the respect of his/her employees, this will have a bearing on the message employees hear when they are given corrective steps. If you respect your boss, you will likely feel remorseful and sad that you've let him/her down. If you don't respect your boss, you'll probably walk away from a counseling session mumbling hard words under your breath, and you'll refuse to believe that you are responsible for any mistake. This will stem from the feeling that the person doing the correcting didn't actually want to help you, but that he/she just wanted to demonstrate power over you.

A single negative correction with no thoughtful follow-up can make employees feel uneasy and scared to come forward in the future to discuss other mistakes. During my career, I learned that whenever I made a mistake, I had to be the first person to communicate it to the bosses, and to take responsibility. It's always better to fix a problem immediately, in order to lessen the overall impact and get back on course as quickly as possible. Also, I learned that people will actually respect you for being the first to admit your faults. Mistakes are an opportunity to demonstrate accountability and maturity in handling them. It might seem counterintuitive, but it's true.

Intimidation, embarrassment, and public ridicule all negatively reinforce bad behavior. *Good* counseling is about creating a healthy environment where all parties are dealt with fairly and discreetly, and having a management team that staff can trust to be consistent in handling disciplinary issues. This doesn't mean that managers push mistakes under the rug, but rather, that they don't show weakness or bias in taking corrective action.

Now and then, a lack of corrective counseling is related to a fear of lawsuits, or of HR's intervention. But human interaction cannot be avoided forever, as we know. So many times, I've seen managers evade controversial conversations,

especially when they are close to retirement; they may not feel like taking the risk with certain employees, especially where ethnicity, gender, or age issues might come into play. Any of these sensitive issues can be used against a company in a lawsuit, even if the manager in question is the same ethnicity, gender, or age as the person who needed to be corrected. This can often make potential counselors feel powerless to address the real problems.

To this day, I remember counseling a female salesperson and her disclosing to me that she felt there was a conspiracy within the organization to have her fired because of her gender. I had known her for a while, and I was always open with her about her performance, which was usually solid, in spite of the occasional human error. This conversation felt much different than those we'd had in the past; she *really* believed that others were prejudicially planning her demise. I didn't believe it, if only for the simple reason that management didn't have the time, cleverness, or expertise to pull something like that off. I didn't know where her fear was coming from, but I knew it was *her* reality, so from her perspective, it was true and important. Of course, I did my homework and carefully observed her work environment to be sure, but I never discovered anything underhanded going on, and she continued to perform well until she eventually moved over to a competitor to take on a larger role. I didn't know how to help her while she was with our company in those final hours, but I *wasn't* afraid to explore the possible gender issue honestly with her.

KEYS TO SUCCESS 🔑 *Chapter 8 Review*

- Never take any **counseling** issue too lightly. Be prepared with all of the reasons for the counseling, and if you're not prepared, *expect* to have a negative outcome.

- Whenever you attempt to correct an employee, be sure to **care** for the person. Right or wrong, take into account the complexities of human behavior.

- You need to display your wonderful **people skills** in order to convey your message to the person you are counseling. It's less about what you say during the session, and more about whether the other person is *hearing you*.

- Everyone is different. Your **understanding** of each person's *maturity level, coping skills, and willingness to be corrected* will be a factor in the success (or failure) of the counseling session. Knowing these qualities beforehand will bring the right words to your mind, and hopefully, bring out the 'right' side of the person you are counseling.

- Most likely, the person being corrected won't remember everything you've said, so always discuss a **follow-up plan** to review points that were made during your session. Don't rehash past issues during the follow up, but do reinforce the positive changes you see in the person's behavior, and do guide him/her onward in personal development.

- Events will happen, so plan for them accordingly, and prepare your staff for future critical encounters. **Nobody is perfect**, and everyone needs correction and guidance—just, in a healthy fashion. We all can stand to make positive changes and to learn from our experiences. Start the **constructive communication** now, and you'll open the door for better interactions later on.

While preparing for a corrective counseling session, keep the above core points in mind. I cannot repeat this enough: The person being counseled needs to feel that management truly cares and that he/she is being heard. If the employee *doesn't* feel both cared for and heard in a counseling session, what kind of result can you expect? I challenge all managers to be more proactive in their approach by creating an open environment for vital communications such as these.

CHAPTER NINE

Plan on People Development

Development is the process of growing, or of being shaped into something more mature or advanced. I'm sure you've heard countless times that people are our greatest assets, but this is only lip service if companies don't take the time to develop their people.

I am a product of the traditional corporate culture. When my bosses wanted to develop me, I was simply moved around from one department or branch to the next—three months here, three months there—and was told to come back after I'd gotten experience, i.e., development. However, *structured development* was absent for the majority of my 36-year career in banking. Down the line, when I was a Senior Manager, I paid special attention to developing others, because I had learned that helping people to broaden their skill sets or move up in line benefited not only those individuals, but also, the company—and therefore, me. So, in this chapter, I want to focus not only on your own Development Plan and on owning your career, but also, on why it's important to help others to maximize their performance.

I don't want to make it sound like all companies *neglect* development. Some companies have the resources to develop their employees through Training Programs. Early in my banking career, I was actually in a Development Training Program created specifically to teach multiple aspects of banking operations. This program gave me the ability to think in terms of multidimensionality, which played a big role in my successful climb of the corporate ladder later on. Another part of the program focused on People Skills for Managers, and these forever changed my effectiveness in dealing with colleagues. In Chapter 3, I mentioned this life-changing course, and how I still use the principles I learned there today.

The problem with *most* training programs of this kind is that, even though they can be helpful, one curriculum doesn't usually fit all; likewise, no company can build an internal Development Program that will meet the needs of everyone it employs. Individual Development Plans (IDPs) have become common practice in the corporate world, but the process and follow-up related to these documents are not always taken seriously. That's why it's very important to take initiative and work with your Management Team to come up with a practical process to develop your own career. Think about what type of support is necessary for your growth, and begin to ask for the things you'll need. Your IDP should be a living document that changes as you change, and evolves as you evolve. You should seek wise counsel to create the right framework for effective development, and you should have conversations with your managers and other mentors to scope out a functional process.

I have a good example of how a well-intentioned Corporate Development Program can still fail certain individuals. I was enrolled in a Leadership Training Program very early on, and at that time, I was told, indirectly, that the Executives used the program to evaluate its future leaders. Basically, I understood that the program made individuals with leadership skills visible to Executive Management, and that it was a pass or fail type situation.

We were selected by our Group Executive and teamed up with peers—so that our teamwork could be assessed. Because so many groups within this company worked in silos, there weren't very many opportunities for interaction before this, so the program was a great way for us to build a network within the company, and to remain close to our coworkers after the program, if we chose to. The groups were then given leadership and other business topics, in the form of problems to solve or new revenue opportunities. By the end of this project period, each group had to give a presentation to Executive Management about its solutions or discoveries. An Executive Sponsor guided the groups and assigned projects, and a Coach was appointed to each group for Personal Development. With all these cooks in the kitchen, to add to the pressure, we were doing all this on top of our other current job responsibilities—which were also being closely monitored for any signs of performance deterioration.

The issue I had with this program wasn't the program itself—it was that this was the *only* opportunity we had to get evaluated by Executive Management for future leadership roles. When I met my assigned team, I realized that 6 out of 10 of us had already been through this wringer multiple times, with the Executives keeping a close eye on their value through several rounds of projects. The remaining 4 of us, including me, were only being given this one-time opportunity for exposure.

I wasn't exactly surprised. This was the environment I worked in. I decided that I would use this experience as an influence to make changes for those under my own Management. Going through this process also helped me to create a better, more robust Development Plan for my employees and for myself. I resolved to make sure that our developments were unbiased, equal, and fair. You can't always control the environment above you in the corporate world, but you can control the one below you.

Another surprisingly positive thing came out of that grueling Leadership Training Program: *I* might not have gotten the visibility I'd hoped for, but with my help, someone else did.

My Group Executive decided to throw a twist into our working dynamic. She had chosen three people for the program—me, a peer, and a next-level-down Manager—and during the first week we were on, she announced that I would be taking over my peer's program responsibilities. The Manager, who usually reported to my peer, now had to report directly to me. This quickly changed everything.

These two women—my peer and the Manager—each had completely different approaches to business and completely different skill sets. My peer resented me for taking over her department, and she sat through the rest of the program hating me. I had had nothing to do with instigating the order of things, but she now had someone to blame. The Manager, on the other hand, immediately began a healthy interaction with me and took steps to us getting better acquainted. She demonstrated the ability to adapt and had the confidence to prosper under any regime. Our Group Executive saw the potential in this Manager, and in turn, she soon gave her more exposure in the company.

When we completed the program, the Manager was assigned a Senior Executive as a mentor, and it was a great piece of fortune. This Executive was open and candid with her. He had two great suggestions: one was some guidance on working under our new Japanese ownership structure and on how to start building strong relationships right away, and the other was advice about women working under women, which had its own elements to consider.

Also, as part of the program follow-up, our Group Executive and Coach reviewed our IDPs. I was allowed to attend the Manager's review meeting, and I saw that the advice given to her wasn't off target. Still, it did not give her enough solid feedback to propel her forward. Fortunately, she and I had forged a bond during the program, and we had a chance to follow up more on her Plan after that.

Years later, following an Executive Management change, the Manager was called up by a new Executive in order to get better acquainted. To her surprise, this Executive encouraged her to strive for Business-Line leadership roles and *not* for Support Management roles. When I heard this, I was glad. She'd won over another benefactor at the highest level. Her Development Plan was working perfectly.

Development is always a process. The Manager in this story owned her career and took every opportunity to work with others, to gain perspective, and to demonstrate the skills she had to succeed. When I left my tenure there and retired, she eventually took over my role at that company. The countless hours we had spent talking and adjusting her Development Plan was time well spent. I am sure she continued to develop herself after I left, and her staff may never know the difficulties she overcame in order to rise the leadership ranks the way she did.

Very few understand a person's internal dynamics and how hard it is to follow a path laid out by another. That Manager's style differed from mine, and her experience was different than mine, and yet, she adapted. Being prepared for transitions—being able to 'reset' oneself according to changes in the organization—is a huge developmental task that not everyone will be up for.

If you plan to move up, or even laterally, within an organization, or if you plan to change careers entirely, your Development Plan will also have to evolve. We discussed how professionals must change at length in Chapter 2. Each phase of your career brings challenges that will reveal your weaknesses and

your strengths, so preparing yourself accordingly requires extreme flexibility.

A saying I had at my old organization was, "I can teach you products, but I can't make you a salesperson." As we'll explore in the next chapter, the same is true of the confidence to lead. Our insecurities, personal maturity, and tenacity are all components of our leadership ability—and no one else can fix those qualities for us. Still, we can benefit greatly from guidance in this regard, allowing others to help us grow when we are lost or unsure. I'll give you a very personal example.

These days, I don't have a boss—and this change is as big as it gets. I spent 36 years familiarizing myself with the regimens of the corporate world, and now, I am a self-employed consultant. Even though I feel like the sky is the limit for me, I know I need to navigate my new non-corporate environment with care, and discipline has taught me that there are both healthy and unhealthy mindsets I could adopt along with my new lifestyle.

I realized quickly that here, on my own, with no one telling me what to do (ha!), boredom can find me more easily. I had been conditioned to the roller coaster ride of corporate life, having occupied dramatic roles at various companies. Most of my retirement process has been about learning how to unwind, while keeping my mind and work schedule active. I must practice moderation, and patience, instead of constantly bracing myself to weather the ups and downs of someone else's company.

"So," I recently asked myself, "what should my Development Plan look like during this time?" I did some soul searching, and then, I started reaching out to some of the people in my network. One day, it occurred to me to request a meeting with a Publicist and a Business Coach, two women I'd met with more than 25 years of experience each. Both listened to my story, and both gave me some sound advice. Their commentary wasn't earth-shattering, but it *was* just what I needed—a dose of useful perspectives on defining my priorities, setting my pace, and gaining a long-view in my new paradigm.

Leadership and sales skills are innate—they are *not* trainable. However, the familiar saying, "You can't teach an old dog new tricks," just won't cut it. You have to do your part—but if you are flexible enough, at least, to take on mentors when needed, you can adapt to anything. Whether you are an employee or an employer, *own* your career, and when you do, accept the support and advice you get from others to further your success. Yes, self-centered competitors and naysayers will always be there, too, but if you stay the course, the growth will be well worth the hardships.

But organizations should also do their part. System-wide Development Planning is more important than ever now, as younger generations join the corporate workforce. Older workers, like me—we who have survived our jobs into our late 40s, 50s and 60s—tend to have the mentality of just doing what we're told and getting it done. No matter our personalities, we adapted to this structure because, during our development, we weren't allowed so much to *question* if we expected to advance. Younger workers, however—in their 20s and 30s—are completely different these days; they want to be actively involved in the company's evolution and to understand their personal development within it. They *don't* just do what they're told, and they don't like being neglected. This is part of the reason why I think they tend to jump jobs every two-or-so years; this movement is part of their Development Plans, and they *do* gain experience with every change. To combat this problem, I'd recommend moving them around within your organization every two-or-so years, instead. Not only might this keep them from leaving, but you'll also end up with valuable, well-developed employees, more broadly capable than Practitioners of the past.

KEYS TO SUCCESS 🔑 *Chapter 9 Review*

- **Development** is the process of growing, or of being shaped into something more mature or advanced. Companies need to develop their people, and you need to develop yourself and those below you in the ranks.

- First and foremost, develop **awareness**, both of yourself, and of others. No Development Plan is complete without the critical skill of being able to observe interactions within a company. Work to be conscious of interdependencies and structural changes, as well as of external opportunities and risks, and Executive Management will start to see you as ready to move up.

- Do strive for **visibility**. Putting your best skills in the spotlight should be part of your Development Plan.

- Make **mentorship** a part of your Plan. Mentor your staff whenever possible, and bring in your own boss or other mentor to give you feedback. If you don't make your Development Plan known, misunderstandings can arise, and important correctional advice can be missed.

- Have **patience**. Development happens slowly over time, and as we mature in life or in our careers, our perceptions also change. What seemed important to you in the past may not be important to you in the future. Snapshots of your Plan in your 20s, 30s, 40s, and 50s will all have very different elements.

- Remain aware of **politics**. Sometimes, there are social (or egotistical) forces at work that can stand in the way of your development. If your Plan continually reaches a dead end, there may be a person outside your control who is responsible for it. In this case, only endurance and *tenacity* can change the tides, as *good fortune, new opportunities, and the support of others* will eventually dissolve all obstacles.

- Above all, learn to **adapt**. Setbacks such as health hurdles, market swings, and other uncontrollable factors will have a bearing on the direction of any person's career. *Evolution* is the key to development.

Remember that regardless of whether your company is able to invest in the development of its employees, *you* are responsible for your own career. Even so, I challenge all employers to tackle the topic of employee development, and to give it importance. If you do, you will be thrilled to see the improvements to your business on the whole as the individuals within it grow.

PART FOUR

Leadership

Earn Trust, Earn Leadership

CHAPTER TEN

Can't Make You into a Leader

The qualities necessary for leadership can be very diverse. According to Wikipedia, **leadership** is a *process* "in which a person can enlist the aid and support of others in the accomplishment of a common task" by using the power of behavioral traits such as intelligence, shared values, and/or charisma. But among a leader's most fundamental qualities is his/her willingness to face unknown risks in pursuit of a vision, motivating groups or individuals toward an objective, no matter what. It's easy to recognize a good leader in the wake of a success, but it's not always as easy to see one in the wake of a disaster. The truth is, not all leaders win every time, and that's what makes those who keep fighting, anyway, *great* leaders. To persevere in the face of defeat and rally people to continue following you with loyalty and trust is <u>true</u> leadership.

Leadership skills are acquired through many experiences and developed over many years. It's not just about being an "alpha," or having a "Type A" personality or a charming smile. Life has to teach you how to be a leader. You may be the boss, but that doesn't mean others view you as a leader. Wealth, privilege, social influence, or some other kind of power can give you leadership status, but without maturity or the right skills, you may not be able to pull leadership off. There's an old saying that if you want to know if you're a leader, look behind you to see if anyone is following; but you should also remember that it's not uncommon to find out later that those following you were driven by greed, fear, blind devotion, or just because they needed to keep their jobs.

Possessing the Elements

Very early in my career, I had the great fortune to work for the President of a retail bank who had admirable leadership skills. Not only did he have charisma and vision, but he also had the wonderful talent of being able to remember the names of all his employees. It was so fascinating to watch the entire company rally behind him with loyalty and devotion. Not all of his tactics were politically correct, but they were all very effective. He had devised one interesting strategy in particular: I noticed he had positioned two talented Executives of equal responsibility under him and pitted them against each other. Both men were very different, but they were similar in their ambition to try and become the next President of the bank.

Years later, I found myself wondering, "Is it wise to pit Executives against each other?" As a leader myself, I understood my boss's tactics. Both Executives were performing at a higher level because of the competitive motivation, and they were also taking some attention off of him; they could be the fall guys, if he ever needed them to be. I had been placed in equally competitive roles in my career, probably in the same effort to push all of us to perform better—and it had worked. The only downside to this strategy occurs when bad leaders use it as a form of manipulation, which ironically, results in lower performance and in trust issues in all directions. Only certain leaders can pull off the competition strategy effectively, and this President was one of them.

As a leader, you need to be consistent in whatever you are doing in order to foster trust and minimize any feelings of favoritism—including and developing *all* of your people. Being a leader involves more than just broadly communicating your vision; it's also about taking the time to visit multiple levels within your organization, familiarizing yourself with each of their issues. They used to call me a "Walking Manager" because when I was in a leadership role, I would make it a point to walk the full floor of the office every day. I wasn't walking around micromanaging—watching over people's shoulders, poking my nose into their business. I *told* them I was walking around to clear my head, or to say "hi" and check up on how they were doing. I was *actually* doing this to give myself visibility, and, to gather information. It allowed me to make changes faster, because I was familiar with all of the issues. But it didn't matter if I was on my own floor, or with the staff in another building—everyone knew that if they approached me, I would listen.

There is another important reason for being visible when you're a leader: Leaders need to lead *by example*. How you treat your staff gets learned and gets passed down—it all starts at the top. Let me give you an example.

One time, I devised an experiment to test my organization for cohesion. I planned an offsite meeting in Huntington Beach at a nice beachfront hotel for my entire group and all of the Support Managers. On the second day, we had a General Meeting planned. The topic of the meeting was Change Management, and specifically, how we were going to change over the next year.

Five minutes into the presentation, I had arranged for hotel security to enter the conference room. We had about 125 people in there, so some noticed that security was standing in the back, but most didn't even see them. Suddenly, I stopped speaking and had the security staff surround the entire group. I regained the group's attention and spoke very softly: "I have arranged for us to take a little trip outside. So, leave everything here, and security will lock the doors and guard our items. Please stand and follow me."

We filed out the side door in a very organized and professional way. I could hear little murmurs from the group, like, "What's up?" and "What's going on?" As we made it out the door, I led them to a bridge that went across Highway 1 to the beach. We all crossed the bridge, and I had them stop on a cement pad surrounded by sand, with a clear view of the ocean.

Once again, I gathered their attention and proceeded to talk about the Change Management Plans. My point was to open their eyes to the fact that unforeseen changes would be coming and a new environment would emerge, but, with the right adjustments and ample trust, we could all move forward beautifully. This experiment worked: it cemented their loyalty, which I had needed to move us forward with the necessary changes.

If we're honest, most people are not trained or equipped to handle the dynamics of leadership. Not everyone is called to be a leader, and there is only so much room at the top. Unfortunately, the norm in the corporate world is that people are often elevated into leadership roles simply because management wants to reward them for hard work, or to keep them around. In my opinion, this isn't really the best approach.

The "**Peter Principle**" was formulated decades ago by "hierarchiologist" Laurence J. Peter, and it illustrates the above point very accurately. Below, the graph shows that leaders who have been advanced based on their past performance in non-leadership roles, and not for their specific abilities as leaders, are often set on a path to incompetence.

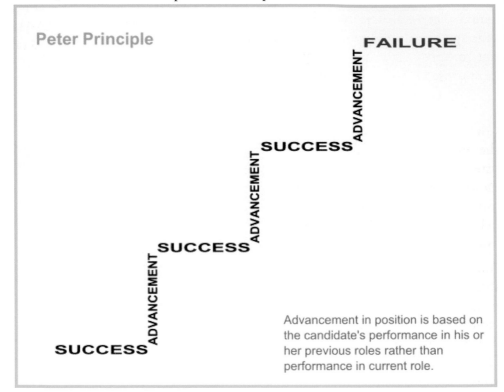

Peter Principle

FAILURE

ADVANCEMENT

SUCCESS

ADVANCEMENT

SUCCESS

ADVANCEMENT

SUCCESS

Advancement in position is based on the candidate's performance in his or her previous roles rather than performance in current role.

This is not to say that if people are elevated into leadership positions they cannot *become* great leaders. But throughout my career, I've watched this Principle in action when dealing with bosses, peers, staff, and even with myself (being able to assess yourself is paramount to being a good leader). A thousand past successes cannot guarantee success in a new leadership position. However, if a person recognizes his/her own limitations, including a lack of developed leadership skills, he/she can change the old game plan to operate at a higher level of competence, and success as a leader is more likely. Unfortunately, no one can change the game plan *for* you—you have to come to that change on your own. This self-initiation is the only thing that transforms being pushed into leadership into a *calling* to lead.

I have participated in countless leadership surveys throughout my 36 years of corporate life, and I have been on both sides of the survey. Employees are usually clear and honest—sometimes even brutal—when rating a boss. I always found it ironic that Executives would survey their staff to find out people's perceptions of their leadership skills—and then when they got the results, they wouldn't enact changes. I'm fond of saying, "Don't send your kids to therapy unless you go first." If you're going to ask for the vote of the people, and you're not going to make changes to your leadership style soon after that, then don't be surprised if your team begins to lose respect for you.

Ownership of Leadership

Owning your role as a leader comes with great responsibilities. You must earn the respect and trust of others. Humility and compassion will move them to listen, and to build a deeper relationship with you. For your part, you should *do* more than you talk about doing. Long-winded and laborious leaders can exhaust their audiences. I've been praised for taking action as a leader, and I believe this is key to earning respect. Leaders must motivate and inspire—not exasperate others with opinions and ideas. Get things done!

Another great leadership skill is the ability to make others aware, and to help them understand the complex tasks before them. Sometimes you need to tell people three or four times what the plan is and why you're doing it, and they still won't grasp it until you're completely exhausted. A good leader has to check his/her communication skills to determine whether the message was clear enough. Did you match your style of communication with theirs so they could receive your message? There will always be people who need a little handholding in the beginning. Picking the right people for the job, so that once they understand the task, they can get it done—*that's* leadership. But even in certain leadership roles, you will not always be blessed with a fully-competent Management Team or the staff to allow you to accomplish the greatest feats you have in mind. What matters then is how you manage the people you have to work with.

Also, leadership isn't exclusive to Management positions; you can be seen as a leader in any role within your company. I can remember that even when I was in Sales, I had to demonstrate leadership skills in order to motivate other Managers and staff to get customers on board by exceeding their expectations. In Chapter 1, I mentioned the importance of Project Managers. Even though he/she is *not* always a permanent Manager, the Project Manager has the role of COO (Chief Operating Officer) on a particular mission, and people must look to that person as the leader for the full course of the plan. A Project Manager needs all of the same leadership qualities that a permanent Manager does.

Chances are that you knew early on in your life whether or not you were predisposed to being a leader. I'm sure there were many events during middle school and onward when people would have begun to recognize you for your leadership skills. But in case you are still in doubt as to whether or not you should be leading, make sure you ask yourself the key questions in the following Chapter Review.

KEYS TO SUCCESS 🔑 *Chapter 10 Review*

- **Leadership** is a *process* "in which a person can enlist the aid and support of others in the accomplishment of a common task" by using the power of behavioral traits such as *intelligence, shared values, and/or charisma*. But among a leader's most fundamental qualities is his/her **willingness to face unknown risks in pursuit of a vision**, motivating groups or individuals toward an objective, no matter what.

- Leaders will *not* always come out on top. It's sometimes hard to recognize a leader whose mission has failed, but the true test of a leader is the willingness to **persevere**, and the willingness of others to keep following.

- Do you *want* to lead? Why? Many are *pushed* into leadership, but few feel that they are really *called* to be in such a role. Figure it out for yourself, and if you must lead, be sure to change your **game plan** as you enter new leadership roles.

- Do you have your **ego** in check? Do you have the skills to develop genuine *trust and loyalty* with people? Without these skills, you'll get mediocre results from drifting, unmotivated staff.

- The **physical appearance** of your communications matter. It's not about gender, race, age, size, or even the way you dress (although, of course, it's best to dress for success and to put your best foot forward at the office). It's more about your *tone and body language*—there's a **humble directness** that people will look for more in your energy than in your words.

- At times, **leadership** *is* **a dictatorship**; there can only be one who makes the final decision. The other side of this is that people need to be able to trust in the power given to you to make the call. The only way to counteract the discomfort of this dictatorship for others is to *earn their respect*.

- Can you handle being questioned by staff, and their asking to always be included? In today's business world, pushback and **inclusiveness expectations** are both common and acceptable.

- Do you have the skills to **train and develop people**? Those you lead will look to you for help with their future progression.

I have another challenge for my readers here—managers, employees, freelancers, artists, or entrepreneurs: Develop the leadership skills necessary, both in yourself and others, to send you and your mentees on a path to success, not failure. My hope is that this chapter helped you to not only evaluate yourself on your leadership destiny, but also, to realize that leadership is about interacting with others positively to get things done. Now, this tip is for the companies: Stop rewarding people with easy elevation into leadership roles, and work harder to assess their real abilities as leaders, and then, to develop them where they are lacking. You wouldn't coach a football game by just throwing in your most eager players; you would send in skilled, prepared, and gifted people with the specific abilities to win. So, play to win. *I* can't make anyone into a leader— but *you* can.

CHAPTER ELEVEN

Patience in Business

Having **patience** in the business world is the ability to accept or tolerate delays, trouble, or suffering without getting upset or angry and making bad decisions. I use the word "ability" because without patience, we would genuinely not be *able* to see things through to the end. You can find countless books, articles, and blogs on patience from the perspective of spirituality or health or stress management. All of them cover the basics, but each is a little different in its execution. In my 36-year banking career, I have seen my fair share of events in which patience, as a skill set, has been applied correctly—I've also witnessed plenty in which it hasn't. Here, I'd like to talk about the skills I've found to be necessary for exercising patience in the workplace. Of course, without patience, you cannot earn trust, and without trust, you cannot earn leadership.

Every day, we fight our reactive instincts in a "microwave culture" of fast results and instant gratification. Even thinking about the word "patience" can trigger agony. The thought of waiting can bring on feelings of worry about unwanted responsibilities and performance expectations. This increases the stress of having to be held accountable. What I'm describing is the pressure that you and others put on you to deliver on projects or to reach certain sales numbers—to demonstrate the tangible signs of progress that should naturally develop over time. Time is money, as the saying goes, and these days, nobody likes to waste a drop of it.

It takes great leadership and maturity to endure through a circumstance that affects the dreaded timetable. Delays are usually a result of a poor scoping of the project—of not having seen it in a holistic way at the beginning, and missing the challenges that lay ahead. Late in my career, I was trained to scope out projects in terms of available talent and resources, and of using these to estimate the time it would take to deliver results. Setting appropriate timelines—allowing for delays while keeping the end in sight—is key to managing expectations. Managed expectations allow us to have patience, so that project hurdles become less about suffering and more about a strategic way of handling circumstances beyond your control. I'll give you an example.

I was once given a bank project to develop a training program for newly-hired Lending Officers. It would be one thing for me to assemble and structure a curriculum, but it would be another to motivate and properly train the participants. The Lending Officers would have to demonstrate the skills they'd learned in my workshops, and they would be assessed by Management to determine if the program was effective. Management wanted measurable results.

In this case, my promptness (good timing) *and* my patience were both needed. Beyond me meeting my deadlines and other objectives, the Lending Officers' performance in the program would actually be out of my control. Still, I knew that if I planned thoroughly, and set up a few measurable milestones, the efficacy of the program would be both quickly and lastingly visible. I created four Key Themes as metrics and incorporated them into the participants' ongoing Performance Review process. I would not get feedback from Management on my program for almost a year, but everyone was able to be patient, because I had shared my own long-view evaluation strategy with them in order to manage expectations. They knew their results were coming, and I knew I had set myself up for success.

In the next chapter, I'll talk more about keeping your cool in trying situations. This involves having the patience to allow a well-formulated structure with honest intentions to play out over time. It's easy to lose confidence when you've overcommitted, when you're not communicating both frequently and effectively, or when you have let incompetence linger on a project. You have a responsibility to monitor and adjust long-term plans, so patience is a matter of knowing when to act and when *not* to—as well as a matter of really *listening* to your people, and trusting that they have the foresight and capabilities to resolve some of the issues along the way. Delays and changes can sometimes actually *improve* your results. What we do with obstacles and setbacks is a test of the resilience of our perspective. We cannot predict or control time, but can navigate it wisely.

Another, much larger test of patience in my career came when I had to oversee my bank's acquisition of a Specialty Market Segment Department. We had a similar Specialty Segment at our bank already, but the new Department was outside of our current footprint; it had more of a national, mid-to-low-end layout and a different sales model.

We did the best we could to scope out the process before and during the acquisition, and we planned long-term goals for the Department. But everything from their logo and their data systems, their pricing and management styles, to their physical location had so many complications that we could not understand the breadth of the problems at the beginning. We knew there were many factors outside of our current control, such as competitor behavior, customer loyalty, and cost add-ons that might come up in the future. Combining our two Specialty Departments into one vision would require, again, good timing, and a mother-load of patience.

We faced unforeseen setbacks from personnel issues and customer impact daily. Luckily, we had great talent in both Departments, and strong overall customer loyalty. I knew that, as a leader, I needed to affect unity in order to maintain momentum. Each time I spoke to Management and staff, I focused on rallying the cause, and I stressed that it wouldn't be easy and that the results wouldn't be immediate, but that we had the chance to become number one in our combined Segment.

But just as we had gotten back on our feet, the bank seized an opportunity to buy out a competitor in this same Segment. The new acquisition would bring in good Management and more loyal customers, but our freshly united Department structure was already being tested. Had we built a strong enough foundation with enough talent to grow *this* quickly? We had established enough patience to watch our original plan unfold, but now, we had added delays and other uncertainties to deal with. Still, I kept on believing that we could be number one, and I chose to believe that the second acquisition would actually further that cause. Again, we would just have to be patient.

The question was how to measure progress while keeping in line with our initial goals under these added conditions. We exercised good Project Management by adjusting our financial measurement milestones. Our clients were key, because they would keep paying our bills, and they could make us sustainable and profitable for the long term. You never get to keep *all* of your customers during this type of acquisition event. Not everyone likes change, and some people are looking for an excuse to leave. Our secret was having an aggressive Client-Acquisition Plan to replace lost customers with new ones, using better pricing.

Our Plan worked, and with patience from all of us, we well exceeded our financial goals. There was still much more to accomplish, but we could be sure that the revenue would be there to help us weather further holdups.

As a leader, having the patience to let a plan evolve to its end state is the ability to endure both internal and external pressure. The politics and ego-related issues that arise during Change Management events like these can consume you. It takes a strong backbone, belief in your people, and the courage to make changes when necessary in order to exhibit this skill set called "patience".

Of course, it's easy to look back after a difficult experience and say, "With patience, it all worked out in the end." How you acted *during* the event is the real test of whether patience was exhibited. Angry outbursts and other emotional responses during difficult times translate into stress for all involved. Stress can suck the life out of you when you are trying to handle an unexpected delay, or to find a solution to some other complication. Throughout this book, I have touched on the importance of having the people skills to care for and develop others. Having patience plays in to this overall strategy, because it's really during times of extreme change that people can best be trained in new skills and perspectives.

Sales, and What Others See

I have been in Sales for most of my career. Timing and patience are big factors when it comes to setting sales goals and the expectations for your results—it's all about: *when?* There is little tolerance for delay in this profession, because it involves people and creates dynamics that are often unpredictable. Ideally, Management and salespeople would like consistent and timely sales, but these are difficult to produce, and patience is always needed. You can drive your organization crazy, and actually lower its results, by being impatient.

One sales situation that requires particular patience is when events on the customer side are driving the process faster or slower than expected (I touched on this in Chapter 6). Another is when new staff is being trained or an outside person is weaved into your organization's structure. An adjustment is always needed to evaluate and improve these circumstances—thus, patience is needed, too.

Patience is not the ability to wait, but the ability to keep a good attitude while waiting.

But patience is also crucial to the basics of Sales. For instance, it's easy to try and rush a specific sale, instead of letting it evolve. Currently, I'm focusing my freelance business activities in Asia, where patience is of utmost importance. A lot of times, a verbal agreement begins with a mutual "yes"—which means that the potential agreement is understood and must now make it through a much larger approval process. If you cut this process short because of impatience—taking "yes" to mean the deal is set, without continuing to build trust by following cultural protocols in order to close it—you will blow the deal and not be invited back for future business.

What you do *while* being patient is the key to your success. Let me give you an example. I was in a department for fifteen years and wanted to move up to a Management position. My boss kept talking about retiring, but this went on for five years longer than anyone expected. I had my hand up to be considered for his position, and I was biding my time. During those five years of waiting patiently, I *thought* that the natural progress upwards for me was to replace my boss—but as it turns out, it wasn't. Just when my five-year wait was over, I got an even *better* position that moved me farther along than I had ever anticipated.

The reason for this surprise was that, during those five years, I continued to perform at my best level, and I took the time to develop more management skills and started planning my future management style. As part of my personal Development Plan, I empowered myself by learning about products, reporting, market segmentation, communication, politics, and of course, People Development (I talked all about Development Plans like these in Chapter 9). I also built a network within the company to help me get things done once I was promoted. The point here is that I didn't just sit and wait. I was proactive in preparing for the next step in my career. It ultimately didn't matter which direction my job would take—I was equipping myself to be a leader. For the ten years following my promotion, I simply executed the Plan I had worked on in those five years of patient preparation.

While perseverance is also essential to leadership, patience is about more than just enduring; it's about the mental and emotional responses you have to life's ups and downs; it's a state of being aware, but still decisive enough to react (reasonably) to what is being thrown at you.

Others can tell by your shared foresight—and your demeanor—whether or not you are capable of being patient. But only *you* can develop patience among your crucial leadership skills.

KEYS TO SUCCESS 🔑 *Chapter 11 Review*

- **Patience** is a *skill set* that can help you avoid making bad decisions by accepting or tolerating delays, trouble, or suffering without getting upset or angry. It is different than **perseverance**, in that it involves your ability manage your own emotions in order to see goals through to their successful end.

- Patience and good timing can help you **manage expectations** when you're working on a project. Patience is almost always about timing—you cannot know the future, but you can plan for unforeseen roadblocks.

- Sharing effective **milestones** with Management is a specific way to manage expectations of fast results, by using a long-view to give them instant gratification in smaller, ongoing chunks. Simply rushing will lower your result, and is never the best solution. Whenever possible, communicate with yourself and others that it'll be OK to wait. **Communication** is vital.

- People are among your **resources**, and they, like everything else, are imperfect — so plan on that! Be realistic more than optimistic. Monitor your team's performance and make corrections when needed. Have patience with them; they do not know everything.

- Have patience with yourself; *you* do not know everything. Count on **setbacks** and delays that even *you* didn't foresee; no plan is perfect.

- Guard your reactions to change by remaining open to it, without creating **stress** when it arrives. A guarded mouth lifts people and does not lower them. Open body language invites feedback and does not repel constructive criticism. **Empower** yourself, and others, to resolve issues confidently. Trust in others to get their jobs done without meddling unnecessarily, and follow up at appropriate and agreed upon intervals to validate progress. Being visibly positive demonstrates a cool and **realistic** perspective. Patience involves understanding the details without having to dwell in them, which can drive yourself and others crazy, lowering performance for all.

The business world has many challenges; that is why it's called "work". Whether you're in a corporate environment or running your own business, you need to be prepared to handle yourself like a leader in every circumstance. All business leaders and staff need a better understanding of the components of patience. As I said at the beginning of the chapter, "patience" isn't usually what people want to hear—especially in the midst of a storm—but it *is* the necessary perspective you must adopt if you want to survive the job.

CHAPTER TWELVE

Controlling Yourself Around Others

Have you ever found yourself losing so much patience with someone—on the brink of blowing up—to the point where you've had to completely shut down, or walk away? This extreme reaction is not unnatural when we deal with difficult people or circumstances. Since we are thrown plenty of frustrations in the workplace, we may find ourselves having these types of encounters throughout our careers. Having healthy relationships with parents and other family members, with mentors, and with close, honest friends can help us learn the tools to maintain our composure—but not all of us have been afforded these blessings.

Especially when in leadership roles, or when dealing with those in charge, it's easier than we'd like it to be to lose **control**—and when I say "control", I mean the ability to exercise restraint, or to keep ourselves in check. This is definitely not a chapter about controlling others; it's about controlling yourself *around* others, especially in tense, hierarchical situations.

As a Part-Time Manager at Sears during college, I had a very difficult relationship with the weekday Full-Time Manager. She'd been there for years, and in her mind, I was a college student—a short-timer—and as such, I should stay out of her way. Thankfully, we had a limited number of encounters due to scheduling, but I do remember a lecture she gave me once that sent me into a rage. She was speaking to me about ordering products and said something to the effect of me needing more time to understand the process. I perceived it as a knock at me being younger and less committed. So, I lost it. No composure, no maturity, no high road—I just blasted her. Well, of course, my boss found out and called me aside to give me some much-needed advice and correction. Thankfully, he knew my sports background and he understood my aggressive nature, so he gave me the criticism in a healthy way. He simply said,

"This is not a high school sports team—it's a business team, and it requires more discipline—so, control yourself."

In Chapter 8, I mentioned that if you trust the people above you, you'll take responsibility for your actions and make positive changes. That's exactly what happened this time. After the Full-Time Manager gave me a few choice words of her own, it was all water under the bridge. She hadn't really batted an eye at my outburst, and with me working to control myself, we worked much better together in the future.

Depth of Perception

What I want to bring to light here is that self-awareness can carry the way. Knowing how you typically react to changes, including disappointments, can help you steer your behavior. Are you typically able to sit through an exasperating meeting, or to stop yourself from cutting short an annoying conversation, or to subdue your body language when you're feeling uncomfortable? An awareness of your skills in these areas can help you hone them.

Strangely, it isn't even usually the current event that causes us to lose it, but rather, it's a build up of prior issues. Venting is a common coping mechanism, and in the right environment, it can be healthy to get things off your chest through conversations with others. I call it a "release valve". Talking it out can help us find a mature way of dealing with our issues. Life is full of surprises, and if you have pent up stress without any coping skills, controlling yourself can become very difficult.

As mentioned in Chapter 5, tone of voice and body language play an important role in how we communicate with others—sometimes, an even bigger role than the words we use. This is a useful area in which to heighten our self-awareness: Are you watching peoples' reactions to your style of speaking and paying attention to their responses? Granted, you cannot communicate *perfectly* in every encounter, and no matter how well you might be dealing with a confrontation, another person's state of mind can skew his/her perception (I could write a book on the topic of "perception" alone). It's most important to simply make an effort to listen better, to acknowledge the other person in *whatever* state, and to take responsibility to control your own emotions. You can never truly know who's on the right or wrong side of a communication, but you can always do *your* part to be open to the possibility that you have changing to do.

Here's a good example of how my own skewed perception of a situation led to a confrontation. While I was a young Assistant Manager in banking, my Manager and three others shared an open space in the branch with me; my boss sat directly to my right. He had a tendency to speak and laugh very loudly, and when he addressed me, it was always with more volume than necessary to get my attention. Finally, I just couldn't handle the tone of his voice anymore, and one day, I blurted out, "I'm not deaf, and you can stop yelling at me." He looked at me in shock, and then he called me over to his desk.

In my mind, I was already filling out the transfer form to leave; I had blown it. I yelled at my boss! He gestured for me to sit down, and then, he leaned forward very close to me. I thought he was going to ream me out, but he just lifted up the hair over his left ear and showed me: there was no ear there! He only had an ear lobe—no ear canal. It was the 80s, and long hair was the fashion for men back then; I had *never* noticed his condition. He looked at me and said, "Sorry, I can't always hear myself." I felt like a moron. Looking back, I could have spent just a little more time in getting to know him better, and I would have caught on to this important issue of his. This was a prime example of my lack of controlling myself, and of how perception plays a huge role in our interactions. I was young and I didn't like being yelled at—and that was my little issue, while his was much more important.

I should address quickly here the art of controlling yourself in your emails. While, as we discussed in Chapter 5, typed communications are often easier to misinterpret, their effects are too often longer-lasting, simply because they are permanent. The person to whom you fired off an angry email that time has those words to refer back to for the rest of his/her life. I've written dozens of inflammatory emails, or responses to other inflammatory emails…and *not* sent them. It's so easy to hit the send button in the moment—but don't. Typing to get something off your chest is a normal way to release the valve, but filling out the addressee field and sending it are unnecessary. Save the email to draft if you feel you need to reference it later on, and when you can, delete it. There's such a powerful feeling in letting your fingers roll out the perfect hard-hitting response, but whether right or wrong, the receiver will see it as an example of your lack of maturity and self-control. (P.S. If you don't know these things already, using Caps Lock in business correspondence tends to comes across like you're yelling, and cc'ing a group when responding to an individual often comes off as an intimidation tactic. If not intended, these choices can look incredibly amateurish; if intended, they usually read as pretty rude.) Writing emails with self-control is just good business etiquette.

Levels of Security

I've mentioned throughout this book how insecurity can derail a good manager or leader. This one quality is a significant factor in why we lose control around others. Insecurity is self-uncertainty, and self-uncertainty, along with a lack of confidence, creates anxiety. This tricky emotional state will always have a negative effect on relationships, both at work and at home.

But how does insecurity manifest itself in the workplace? Well, one sign of it could be avoidance or isolationism; conversely, someone might display an overly-controlling personality (micromanagement style) among his/her defense mechanisms. Insecurity is different than humility, which involves recognizing one's shortcomings while maintaining a healthy dose of confidence and self-esteem. Insecurity involves being unable to objectively evaluate one's abilities, and instead defaulting to an emotional interpretation of events. Any two people working together might have entirely different levels of insecurity.

We cannot control other people's insecurity issues, just as they cannot control our behaviors—but you *can* look into your own condition before dealing with others. We all have a little insecurity in us; it's our degree of awareness around it that either moderates or unleashes negativity towards others.

A boss I had towards the middle of my career provides a good example of the negativity unleashed by unbridled insecurity. This boss consistently used intimidation to force others to comply with his will. There were three other men and one woman on his team, and he delighted in pushing all of them to the point of tears during his staff meetings. It made him feel powerful—which helped him to mask his insecurity (or so he thought). I had to accompany him on his customer calls, and to go on several business trips with him. He liked to stay at very ritzy hotels, so the trips were tolerable for me, except that I was forced to have dinner with him. One night, I remember noticing the irony of dining with him at the Santa Barbara Rivera district, overlooking the bay as a cruise ship came to port for the evening. This was the first time a cruise ship had been in the harbor in over two decades, with fireworks and everything. I remember looking over at him and thinking: *how romantic, just with the wrong person.*

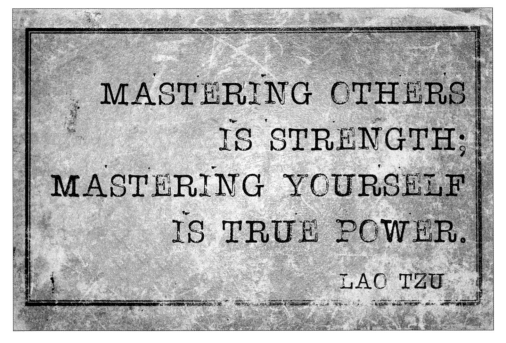

MASTERING OTHERS IS STRENGTH; MASTERING YOURSELF IS TRUE POWER.

LAO TZU

Shortly after this trip, my boss made a move to establish more control over me. He called a closed-door meeting with me and proceeded to tell me that the only reason I was allowed to travel and stay at nice places and keep my job was because of him. I'd had enough by then, of course—so I lashed out.

"I am not your 'yes' man like the others here, and I have earned my job," I said. I got up and slammed the door as I left his office. It was a week before we spoke again. We had an unavoidable encounter as we walked by each other in the hallway. My boss looked me in the eyes and gave me a quick, "We ok?"

I should have been conciliatory, but instead, I let my immaturity take over yet again. I was too defiant this time, and gave him more strong words to set the boundaries on how I expected him to deal with me from now on. Although I felt better standing up for myself than not, I'd just created even more insecurity for both of us to deal with in the weeks that followed. Even when dealing with hostile individuals, guarding your mouth is the most important thing you can do to preserve your working relationships—and your own sanity.

Setting the Tone

When dealing with those under you, it's important to keep in mind your temperament when you're confronted with sensitive issues. Using an arrogant, lording, or even dismissive style shows a lack of professionalism. Remember, your employees are all watching your patterns and looking for replicability. In other words, they are learning your style, and crafting their own approach for dealing with *you* in the future.

A great place to start bringing awareness into how you can control your own behavior as a leader is during a group or staff meeting. This affords you the opportunity to see how other participants interact and behave with each other. I took a course once on Group Dynamics and learned a few helpful tools that can make way for more healthy interactions in a group setting. They are:

• Have an agenda, but be open to changes.

• Get to know the group members outside of meetings; this is where **trust** is developed.

• Manage time; people do not like having theirs wasted.

• Move people back onto topic quickly when they are diverted.

• Assume people are prepared for the sake of those that are; regurgitation kills enthusiasm.

• Let those who are unprepared catch up. Leaders need to monitor participation and the meeting of requirements by different group members.

• Never wait longer than 3 to 5 minutes to start a meeting. If delayed, create a useful dialogue to soothe the crowd.

- Listen. You are not the only speaker.

- Move topics off the table if more information is needed to discuss them. (Be consistent with your follow-up, and plan future meetings for the tabled issues.)

- Make sure materials are delivered for review in advance to the entire group; never send them something just before or at the meeting.

- Look for attentiveness in your participants. Are they working as a team to move forward, or are they a group of people that are just giving lip-service to one another?

- End the meeting on time—people *do* make other plans.

But you should also be aware that sometimes, forces outside the workplace will affect your self-control. Family issues like divorce, poor health, and financial conditions can come with you into the office, whether you mean them to or not. These life circumstances often create misplaced anger that can lead to confrontation. Unfortunately, home life and work life are intertwined, and personal events have a bearing on how you are able to handle yourself in both environments.

It's also crucial to note that there is no essential difference between how men and women can control themselves. This is *not* a gender issue. We all have stress buttons that can cause us to respond to situations in a negative manner, but without a doubt, bosses get away with poor behavior much more than employees do. Not just here in the US, but in many cultures, entitlement can yield a bit of behavioral wiggle room—I've seen this play out time and time again, with both males and females. The human power culture is universal.

So, here's a short story about a leader losing composure. I've seen the best lose it, and I've lost it, too. When your agenda is more important to you than the people involved, it can push you to lose your temper whenever you are confronted with opposition. I once attended a well-orchestrated strategic meeting held by a team of consultants our Executive had hired to lay out statistical examples of problems that warranted my company's correction. But the personal agenda of the Executive was so apparent in their presentation, and the information so slanted, that the entire audience saw right through the plan. At the meeting, I can remember pressing the consultants to consider the implications of the statements they were making.

The Executive jumped in. "What do you mean? The numbers are correct!" she defended.

I actually love how open (and sometimes combative) conversations can help us find better solutions, but I've also seen this backfire when either party's tone becomes domineering. Ultimately, the audience starts losing trust in the leader. Never think you can fool people when making suggestions in either a forceful or an underhanded way. Hidden motives almost always become apparent through some signal in your communication.

I restated my observation that if you looked one level down, their story would look radically different than their current summary. This was the last thing the Executive wanted to hear. We all spent the rest of the meeting watching her try very hard to control the reveal of her secret agenda, and sliding right off the cliff. In this case, it might have served our leader to know how to face stressful situations without losing her composure.

KEYS TO SUCCESS 🔑 *Chapter 12 Review*

- Especially when in leadership roles, or when dealing with those leading you, **controlling yourself** amounts to the ability to exercise restraint, or to keep yourself in check.

- Learning to be a **better listener**—and not an individual that has to speak all the time—is a great exercise of self-control. Try listening to a complete conversation before blurting out your point. How often do you start formulating your response when someone else has just gotten started? Keep doing this, and you're sure to miss out on all the real points.

- People do seek out weakness in order to control others, so familiarize yourself with these types of conversations, and do not allow yourself to be provoked into acting out. Find healthy ways to vent—**"release valves"**—in order to discharge negative feelings before they explode.

- Treat others with respect, even when they don't deserve it. Have someone to hold *you* accountable. This support structure helps to monitor your behavior by providing safe **feedback.**

- Practice patience *and* perseverance; they are different and equally important leadership qualities. The truth always comes out eventually, so while you might not be vindicated by every **communication** in the moment, believe in yourself and *not* in the negative comments. Still, be willing to take criticisms and make changes. The truth will set you free from reactivity.

- We humans are a protective species, so when you feel attacked, watch your mouth. What are you defending? It's probably not worth it to lose your temper. Since **perceptions** can be skewed by personal events, remember that in spite of your best intentions, there is always a possibility that you might be in the wrong.

You own your actions and reactions at work, so be aware and be honest—about yourself most of all. Be willing to address any inappropriate outbursts you may have right away. It can be extremely difficult to mend relationships and rebuild trust, even after a single instance of losing self-control. You have to earn trust to earn your call to lead, so do your best to make constructive interactions with others more important than your emotions in the moment.

PART FIVE

Legacy

Leave a Legacy

CHAPTER THIRTEEN

Focus on the Future

One of the issues with the predominant expediency of today's world is that it encourages very little thought about the **future**. We have a tendency to look at the immediate issues in front of us and to neglect long-term planning—the development needed for truly sustainable and profitable enterprises. By now in this book, we've covered much of what it takes to be a leader, but I wrote this last part to challenge you to make efforts to look *beyond* your current role, even as you face the everyday issues in your career. Only by looking ahead can we hope, as bosses, to leave a proud work legacy behind.

I have coined a little phrase, which applies to the forward-thinking mindset I'm stressing here: "Plan to be spontaneous." This means you should be prepared to adjust your plans even when they're going well, and to have the knowledge to choose wisely when to make changes. All plans, whether short-term or long-term, are subject to uncertainties. These might come up around the people you hire, the products you buy or sell, or the overall business models you design and promote. Planning and developing strategies that operate successfully in both the present *and* the future can be tricky. It's key that we learn the ability to look beyond what is known and press ourselves to understand how we'll manage future events. In other words, just as we cannot control others, we cannot control the future—but in all cases, we *can* control our own ability to adapt.

Let me explain further how to adapt a business model. The leadership of any enterprise relies on its people to manage change by staying in tune with the customer base—while heeding current regulations and economic circumstances—in order to adjust smoothly. This adaptability, or scalability, has to be embedded in the company's DNA so that it can stay relevant and continue to add value to clients and investors, as well as retaining its number of useful employees. Scalability amounts to the ability of a business to maintain or increase profitability as the volume of sales grows or shrinks.

There was a time in my career, while serving with two other Executives (one was my boss), that we took on the task of recommending changes to a Support Department that wasn't under any of our direct supervision; it was called the Commercial Customer Service Unit. This segment supported my markets and others, and it was a fairly vital part of the business. I was told that the other two Executives would consider my suggestions, but that a vote would be required to approve and implement them.

One thing about planning for the future is that it always helps to first look back into the past. History teaches you valuable lessons in its stories of wins and losses—of whether or not a company has handled past changes successfully, or of whether it has failed to adjust before. I had to take a good look at the history of this Service Unit. As it turns out, the Department had drifted so far from its original design—which had been quite scalable—that it had become unrecognizably rigid, dysfunctional, and costly. Not only had it lost sight of its initial vision, but also, its Managers had consistently failed to communicate or to make changes when vital. I asked myself this question: What was the original purpose and structure of this Department, and was that business model primed for success? Management had been so consumed with current difficulties that it was failing yet again to recognize how its foundation was faltering. It was ironic that so many customers continued to say the Department was valuable, but that they were disappointed with the current service levels. Those service levels should have clearly indicated the internal trouble.

My immediate recommendation was to scale back the structure of the Department so that it would once again adhere to the more flexible model it was aiming for decades ago. The staff would need to be overhauled to better access their skills, so they would have to undergo one round of firing and hiring, including Management. My goal was to bring back the expertise, reliability, and overall value of the Unit, both by adapting now, and by reformatting for future adaptations.

The initial scaling-back of the Department that I was suggesting would make it immediately less of a cost burden for my company. But to me, it was much more important that the business model again become more scalable, as originally intended. This would lend itself more easily to our tracking activities and measuring effectiveness; other systemic problems and anomalies could at last be identified and addressed.

The future of this Department was also important to our company's customer retention, but the cost seemed to be a bigger concern for the Executives than getting the structure right. After I'd made my recommendations, all three of us took the vote on whether or not to implement my strategy. They both voted in favor of *not* implementing my business model.

Instead, in an attempt to handle the cost issues promptly, I watched over the next few years as a complete turnover of the existing Management in that Department took place. There was an equally high turnover of the other staff, as the quality of our Commercial Customer Service continued to deteriorate. The present staffing and money problems were being addressed—sort of—but there was no careful eye on how to bring it all back together.

I shared this example because I wanted to show you that the scalability and durability of a business model is imperative to creating an enterprise that will be sustainable. Future thinking pays off when the design and structure of a business model accommodate those concerns that haven't yet become pressing. This isn't a new concept in the financial, manufacturing, or retail sectors. If a company is losing money and not growing, it's normal to see cuts; but for growing companies, it's important to have sound Structural and Communication Plans in place to make future adjustments without having to simply lose a lot of staff. Economic cycles prompt many companies to expand or shrink, whether this was planned for or not. Having a *scalable* business model is just one of the ways that a company can prepare for unforeseen events.

Oftentimes, Management can be almost brain dead in regards to preparing for future changes. I always suggest "looking up, not down" at issues, but many Managers are so overworked (or incompetent) that they cannot see the bigger picture. Or, sometimes, they just don't want to ask themselves how their current decisions are going to affect their short- and long-term objectives. People only know what they know, and they cannot always see beyond that point.

In my past life as an Executive Banker, I participated in government Stress-Test Banks. In 2012, the new Dodd-Frank Act required OCC Stress-Testing practices for all National Banks (the FDIC had similar requirements for Community Banks) to measure if they had enough capital to withstand the impact of adverse developments. The extreme-stress scenarios they put us through ranged in magnitude from global events, to earthquakes and terrorism, to civil unrest, to high unemployment, to mere interest-rate fluctuation. The act of modeling these events on the Balance Sheet was a feat unto itself; I watched the finance people work countless hours just to illustrate imaginary results. I had the easy job—I just had to predict the magnitude of the changes to the Liability side of the Balance Sheet for Commercial Deposits and Fee-Related Income.

Future-thinking most certainly came in handy for this assignment. Luckily, the business model I worked under had been developed decades ago and was built to withstand economic cycles by having different business sectors counterbalance the positive or negative changes that might occur over time. It was a brilliant model, created by a Senior Executive who understood the importance of durability; he was an engineer by training, but he knew how to craft a sustainable business model. Our structure allowed me to have a more realistic view when answering the hypothetical questions that were presented during the Stress Test. The model also demonstrated that there would be minimal impact as a result of most of the scenarios they were throwing at us. A business can survive any test or trial—even those of Biblical proportions—with the right planning.

But while you're focusing on the future, you shouldn't neglect the present any more than you should forget the past. I've seen Management spend so much time analyzing future risks— coming up with hypothetical economic and business cycles and discussing possible pitfalls—that the current issues are completely ignored. Preparing for unknown contingencies can feel all-consuming, but in order to lessen these possibilities, you need to limit the number of shaky variables. It's better to remain nimble than to over-prepare; you can buy *too* much insurance or *too* many hedges, for instance, in trying to protect yourself against every imaginable future event, only to discover you have no money left.

The Three Virtues

Do not forget, either, that People Development plays a crucial part in the future of any company. I want to focus here on harnessing three virtues in yourself and in others—**perspective**, **creativity**, and **resourcefulness**. These virtues allow your organization to stay flexible and to avoid stagnation. In terms of People Development, you can maximize on these virtues by hiring the right people now and retaining them for later. Remember that the talent you develop today will go on to manage the evolution of your business model, and they will help you to stay efficient far into the future.

It's hard to find people with all three of these virtues, so if you possess them personally, or you have people on your team who do, thank your lucky stars. If you aren't so lucky, then you either have to create a plan to improve yourself in these areas, or you have to hire new talent that exhibits these qualities. This all stems back to being aware of your own unique strengths and weaknesses in order to gain an edge on future success.

Diversity of thought—having multiple perspectives—can play a big part in successful planning. If you surround yourself with people who are just like you, you'll only get one perspective. The secret recipe for staying fresh is to hire people with a mixture of different experiences, and to encourage them to challenge you and each other, and to always bring forward their concerns and suggestions. One of the best ways to test yourself for future durability is to hire younger employees. The younger generations are often more in tune with information that can affect

your future than are more seasoned professionals. The youth in your organization are going to end up doing the company's bidding, and their insights will allow you to start building models that can stay flexible to changing market patterns.

Let me illustrate an example of the value of the youth **perspective**. At one point in my career, I was blessed to have been able to hire a young Analyst to help me with strategy. She was in her twenties and was not a Strategist by trade, but she'd graduated from Wharton Business School and had gained experience with Morgan Stanley, as well as with a large talent agency in Los Angeles. During our initial interview, she showed a unique inquisitiveness and strong skill set for challenging the status quo. I knew that the status quo served no purpose in my job, and that what I needed was someone to challenge me not to live in the past. She seemed like just the person for this task.

At the end of our interview, she told me a story about a previous employer who had once thrown a pencil at her during a staff meeting. When I offered her the job, I jokingly included in the terms of the contract that I would never throw a pencil at her. We worked together very well. I had her listen to my visions, and she would come back to me later with an interpretation of them. This gave her time to research her ideas and to put extra thought into my plans for the future. She wasn't afraid to give me pushback on many topics, and it really made me think about the visions I shared with her.

Future-planning is not only a Manager's responsibility. Those who are in support roles, in any capacity, must voice the unseen issues that can weigh an organization down. Executive Management, in most cases, has respect for employees that look into the future and come up with answers that are simultaneously realistic and thought-provoking (sparked with **creativity**). For those of you who work under short-sighted Managers, who ignore the holes in core strategy, or worse, place patches over them—my heart goes out to you. Nothing can be more frustrating than working day after day on recurring issues, with no future-fix in sight. As a Manager, staying fresh by remaining open to new ways of doing things, is vital when preparing for what's next.

But staying fresh isn't always easy. You'll find that others in your organization will not understand the need to keep varied perspectives around. People love to stick with their textbook formulas and methods, even when the exact opposite is needed to define visions that will stand the test of time. This is not to diminish proven practices, but to point out that it's imperative to introduce creativity into your business in order to stay relevant in a fast-changing environment.

Another crucial factor in future-planning is having the **resourcefulness** to adjust—quickly—to short-term issues. Simply being aware of internal or external fluctuations is not an excuse to be stagnant for the moment. In the case of the competition, for instance, it's not enough to observe the potential threat; you cannot let others in your market imitate or outmaneuver you, or you'll lose your value in the long-term.

During the last decade of my career as an Executive, I started refocusing the strategy in my Sales organization annually, so that we'd be better prepared each and every year. We spent the third quarter of each year on analysis, and then, on developing plans for the year to come. We spent the last quarter of each year making the changes necessary to be running full-steam again by January 1st. At times, we addressed changes in the competition, redirecting our focus to future sales opportunities. We also made personal changes by introducing new or revised products for our customers, or by working to improve talent. Each year, I altered Management roles to help adjust to the events already in process, but also, to adapt to future circumstances. When moving staff around, it's all about placing people in roles that will create more options (flexibility) as you further your company's cause in its new direction.

Communication Plans are particularly vital to managing the future, because change will test everybody, so your flexibility as an organization will be hampered if anyone is left out of the discussion. As we discussed in Chapter 12, placing regular milestones along the way can help you not only to assess the progress you're making in whatever new direction you've chosen, but also, to get buy-in from your staff. If, on the other hand, you want to assess whether the people *above* you are properly planning for the future, ask them questions. Pay special attention to the answers Upper Management gives you. If the responses are weak, apologetic, or absent—if you get an, "Oh, I forgot about that," or a long, awkward pause, instead of a forthright reply to your concerns—it will be very obvious whether much thought has gone into the topic at all.

Thinking ahead should give you the confidence to lead, even without help from above. You might not have all the answers to all of your questions, but if you do your part to bring out the virtues in your sector, you and your staff can prepare to face those answers head on when they reveal themselves. Do you accept my challenge, as a Manager or as an employee, to look into your future? Find out whether the business model you are currently creating or working under is sustainable. Don't just assume that you'll have the flexibility later to withstand unknown obstacles. You have to build flexibility in from the start, because when it comes to change, it's not a matter of "if" it will come—it's only a matter of "when."

KEYS TO SUCCESS 🔑 *Chapter 13 Review*

- Our culture of expediency makes us forget to look to the **future**. But in business, future-planning is necessary. Your goal here is to prepare to be as *flexible* as possible, or, in other words: "Plan to be spontaneous." This is the only way to foster **sustainability** for your company.

- Remember, you can't **control** the future any more than you can control others, so don't neglect the *past* or the *present*. You can spend so much time analyzing future risks that the current issues fall through the cracks. Don't waste time planning more than 5 years out.

- Mistakes practice, and practice makes perfect. You need to understand the cause and effect of past experiences to make sure you are not letting **history** repeat itself.

- Harness the **Three Virtues**. Sometimes we need outside **perspective** to help us think beyond our limited view of the world. Life is about change, and change needs to be considered **creatively** in order for your work to stay relevant. You and your staff will need to be **resourceful** in tending to the issues you observe, even if it seems like those issues are currently small potatoes.

- Never forget about **People Development**. The Virtues in which you are lacking can be developed in others. Staff turnovers can affect your progress, but *scalable* and *durable* **business models** with carefully managed *talent* can grow your legacy.

- Building in **milestones** is a great way to be sure you can stop and assess what changes are needed at regular intervals. You should schedule future reviews to make adjustments whenever possible.

- Make sure your **Communication Plan** about the future takes all players at all levels into account. Get everyone in the organization, both above and below you, to **buy in** that changes will be needed, especially in regards to both *costs* and *structures*.

- What will happen to your goals for your organization if you leave? The future should yield success, even without you there; *plan* **for succession**.

CHAPTER FOURTEEN

The Torch You Light, Carry and Pass On

Leaving a **legacy** as a boss means that you've successfully passed on your words or behaviors through the interactions you've had over the course of your career. I've seen people leave both good and bad legacies—either can add a lasting impression in other people's memory banks, equivalent to an inheritance (wanted or unwanted) in the physical world. You leave plenty of legacies behind you in your personal relationships, as well as through your successes and failures in business. You *must* consider the impact you'll have on others throughout your life.

A non-physical legacy can't be measured in dollars, but it can be extremely valuable. Yes, financial results can also be recognized as a legacy, but numbers in and of themselves cannot make a legacy truly strong. Think about leaving financial resources behind without having organized strong human capital to manage those resources. Then, think about a learning experience you've given someone as a mentor. It's the lessons you've taught, the time you've given, and the opportunities you've provided others that I want to remind you of before this book is done.

One of the best examples of a legacy I've witnessed was former President Reagan's 1997 speech—this was one of the two times in my life that I got to see and hear him in person. This second time, at a Bakersfield business conference, the event was unforgettable. Before the former President got up on stage, a famous impressionist named Rich Little did impersonations of Johnny Carson, current President Bush, Ross Perot, Nixon, Clinton, and then, Reagan. Just before Little's impersonation of President Clinton, he said, "Let me imitate another president," and then, he stopped, and said, "Ladies and Gentleman, Hillary Clinton!" The crowd went nuts. When Little arrived at his impersonation of Reagan, he walked slowly to the center of the stage, then gave the "thumbs up" sign and placed his hands on top of the podium as he stepped up to it. He even gave that little tilt of his head, and the familiar "well" that always warmed the crowd. His imitation of Reagan was uncanny and the audience loved every bit of it, especially knowing the real thing was soon to follow.

When the time came at last, the MC introduced Reagan, who came to the center of the stage, walking slowly to the podium, placing his hands down on top of it, and tilting his head. He then paused for what felt like a couple of minutes, exchanging a long, playful gaze with the audience. Finally, he spoke: "Are you glad to see the real man?"

The crowd erupted into laughter, but the former President took them back down to serious in seconds; we were soon hanging on his every word. In my opinion, we had been aimless as a nation before President Reagan. He led us into a different era, one which saw major changes in our relationships with both China and Russia as a result of his leadership. Of course, both of our country's political Parties—including the Democratic Speaker of the House—helped Reagan accomplish these changes. As he spoke now at the event, you could hear in his voice the conviction he had always had about his beliefs, and equally, his genuine care for others—his humility. This speech was one small emblem of the legacy he had built over decades, with the aid of his closest colleagues and supporters.

Through humility, others can know and recognize a great leader. The ability for you to remain people-oriented, rather than self-centered, is a trademark approach for leaving a good impression. Humility comes from your mistakes and your recoveries, and also, from those you've learned from and have taught—all of the people who count. It is sad when some people look back over their lives to see what appears to be a legacy of success, and yet, they lack the sensitivity to admit that others helped them get all the way to the end.

I also know that some people lay out a Legacy Plan to try and ensure they will leave a mark, but I'd argue that since we can't know the future (and not everything will always go our way) this approach is short-sighted. We don't, in most cases, get to *plan* on leaving a legacy; rather, our legacy develops over time as a result of our [mis]adventures, and is then left behind us, whether we like it or not. Whether you are a stay-at-home mom or a CEO of a multinational company, you have an impact on others. The ongoing changes and struggles in life give you all the Opportunity and Exposure you need to leave a legacy.

Daily, you make decisions that affect yourself and others, both on a personal level and in your professional endeavors (i.e. in Mentorship and other Leadership roles). Each one of these decisions demonstrates how well you respond to changes and address challenges, and this plays the predominant role in how others view you.

When we endeavor to take an objective and honest look at our legacies, our view would be distorted without input from others. As a protective species, we guard ourselves most fiercely, which can often result in under- or over-valuing our personal strengths and weaknesses. I learned long ago that if you want to see how you are *really* doing, you should ask your kids, your spouse or partner, or your close friends for feedback. Openness and inclusiveness to and of others' perspectives is vital to seeing—and developing—the 'real you'. How often to do you converse deeply with others, though? Do you interact in a diverse way all of the time, or only when you have to? I ask these questions to illustrate that, among our many actions, communication defines our legacy.

I have addressed many Management Development topics in this book, including the various skills you need to be a good leader or Manager. You may have noticed that a few of these abilities became thematic; among the most important are self-awareness, a focus on others, and being both discerning and flexible in the face of uncontrollable events. Your core responsibilities as a boss are to develop the needed people skills and to acquire the emotional stability to deal with whatever comes your way.

Actions Outlast Words

As I mentioned, both good and bad legacies can be left behind us. So before I leave you here, I want to talk more about how our actions play a role. While people *do* often cling to words more than they should, actions are what matter in the long run; only these leave tangible effects whether the power of words lasts or fades.

While I was wrapping up the writing of this book, I took several of my close friends to the Ronald Reagan Library in Simi Valley. I wanted to share the impact Reagan has had on me with some people I care about. The friends I brought this time came from diverse backgrounds: they were two women who recently moved here from Beijing, and an All-American gay couple. I figured that if a varied group could collectively show interest in this man, it would be a good test of his legacy.

By the end of the day-trip, all four of my friends agreed that Reagan had been a great and trustworthy leader who had truly excelled in influencing others while upholding a humble communication style. One of the guys in the couple had met Reagan at the White House when he was a boy, and he told us the story of that experience with admiration in his voice. Later, during dinner, our continued analysis of his Presidency made clear to our group that Reagan hadn't always pleased everyone (nor had he tried to) but that he must have had a basic belief in the good of all people. We all agreed again on this point; his legacy for all of us was how he had championed others.

But really, leaving a legacy is *always* about other people—how you impacted them with your choices, either directly or indirectly. To wrap up my numerous Reagan examples, I think of his taped speech that used to play inside the Oval Office Room at the Ronald Reagan Library. In this speech, he spoke about how, out of respect, he never took his jacket off in the Oval Office. His belief was that he was there to do a job for the nation, and that while on that job, he must always do the right thing, whether others were watching or not.

Over the course of my own career, I've always held myself to the standard of the successful legacies left behind by some of the greatest leaders. Reagan and others like him have clearly influenced me significantly, and this has led me to continually focus my attention on giving back. I've also admired the adaptability of the greats, so I've learned that no matter what the landscape of my own life looks like at any given time, I should remain humble and respectful.

There's no better way to assess the value of someone's legacy than to look at the results. But these could be strictly performance-based (monetary, for instance), or, they could be more about innovation, or reputation. As I mentioned in the previous chapter, I learned many years ago from working with bankers in Capital Markets that there is no hedge that guarantees no loss, just as there is no insurance that covers all replacement costs. In other words, since everyone has a different expectation of what great results should or could look like, all legacies are subject to scrutiny and disappointment. So, the best way to assess legacy based on the outcomes is to be equally flexible about what those results actually are in a particular case. Perhaps, a boss ran into too much pushback during his time at your organization, but you noticed that the creative adjustments he had begun to make were responsible for the success of your business later on. Maybe, the numbers won't fully capture how good of an experience that boss created for her employees, and how smoothly the company began to run after her tenure there.

People are commonly remembered for igniting change. This is a great torch to light and to carry as a leader. Even after you are gone, others can look back at the before-and-after and see clearly whether the impact of your performance was good or bad. If the changes you started were beneficial, you will have formed a very positive legacy for yourself. If the changes were detrimental, you will have forged a bad legacy instead.

Unfortunately, it is difficult to detect the legacy you are leaving while you are still in the midst of your journey. You cannot always gage from outward reactions how people truly feel about the changes you are bringing about. You can only spend time listening to them, and doing your best to hear (sometimes beneath their words) what value they are placing on the changes happening around them.

In Chapter 5, I mentioned an altercation with a work peer that left me bewildered. When I got moved up in the ranks at that company, this Manager told me that my bad reputation had preceded me—she did not value the work

We Are The Legacy
We Leave Behind!

I had done. In my past position, I had built a legacy over 17 years that I *thought* was in good shape, but as it turned out, she and others in her Department felt I'd negatively impacted them.

But the real problem, I determined, was that I had not spent *any* time with this peer over those 17 years; the only feedback she had gotten about me was from her people. I realized then that if I alienate others, even accidentally, a bad reputation will form over time that can eventually ripple out even larger after I've gone.

We do bump and bruise each other sometimes at work, figuratively speaking. This is a common occurrence at any office that we must embrace, since we face similar people and processes as obstacles to our getting things done. Many times, we won't even get to meet the people we are affecting the most. They'll never really know us, or get to see our pure and impure intentions—our level of interest in others, including them, or what our decisions are (and why) behind closed doors. We can learn so much just by interacting with our work peers as much as possible.

Life is not perfect, and so our business life will always have its challenges—the people we work for, work with, or employ; our customers and vendors; the government and the economy. Develop the agility to manage well under pressure, and to make solid decisions in spite of chaos. No matter what, you have to **trust** *yourself* on the job—that you're working to the best of your abilities, and that your intent is good at the core. *We* are not perfect, and people affected negatively by us will in most cases view our decisions as personal, even when they're not at all. You have to stay the course, and if your intentions are, in fact, professional, you will leave a legacy of professionalism. That inner torch of self-assuredness casts an incredible light on your employees, and your mentees, especially; trusting your actions and remaining bold in taking them is the greatest torch you can hand off to others.

KEYS TO SUCCESS 🔑 *Chapter 14 Review*

- Leaving a **legacy** as a boss means that you're passing on your words—or, more importantly, behaviors—through the countless interactions you have in the course of your career. Your employees and your **mentees**, especially, need you to do this with a bold <u>**trust**</u> in yourself if they are going to trust *you*.

- Look back at the shadow of your words and actions, not to dwell in the past, but to learn from your experiences. In forward-planning, think about both the **sustainability** of the *changes* you are rooting for and the measurability of your *results*. These are important factors that can be looked at to assess the overall **value** of your legacy.

- How are you incorporating people into your process—and how are you treating them? Your **reputation** depends on your being inclusive. Do you transmit a "We all did it!" communication-style to reward those who help you in any way? Remember that you never get somewhere alone. You can make an impression by giving credit to others whenever it is due.

- Planning a legacy is usually futile, but you should *always* plan on exceeding **expectations**. Simply meeting goals is acceptable, but great legacies are left via exceptional results. All the same, you can't please everybody, and many will only see the worst. Decide which friends and co-workers you trust the most, and weigh in with them when you receive harsh criticisms from others.

- Even when you trust your actions, you must be the first in **humility** to admit mistakes. This does not make you weaker, since the human condition is that we are not perfect. Look at yourself honestly to determine your own motives.

- Above all in business, be ready to move on. You cannot change the past and you cannot know the future. Life continues, and we need to **live powerfully in the present.**

Like I said, most of us don't plan on leaving a legacy, but one materializes for us whether we like it or not. Your impact on people can either be fruits of labor to nourish all of your careers, or snakes to poison and take all of you down. In reality, your legacy will probably be a mix of good and bad. For instance, a micromanager with bad people skills can nonetheless develop others to succeed. A legacy can be a double-sided coin—one side might be demonstrative or histrionic, while the other side might be genuinely focused on helping others prosper. You, along with all of your defects and assets, will determine your legacy.

Hopefully, this book has brought you an increased awareness of the rippling effect your behaviors have on others. Be bold, take measured risks, treat people with respect, and foremost, strive to make the best of wherever or whatever your position in your career is at this very moment. When you look back on your own legacy, you'll realize it was shaped by every single person you shared an experience with along the way.

ABOUT THE AUTHOR

Les J. Goodwin

PRESIDENT/CEO, ISE ADVISORY GROUP, INC. (US)
MANAGING DIRECTOR, ISE ASIA ADVISORY GROUP PTE LTD. (SINGAPORE)

In 2014, Les Goodwin founded the consulting firms ISE Advisory Group, Inc. (ISE) and ISE Asia Advisory Group, Singapore to provide business support and expertise in Strategic Planning, Project Management, Human Capital Assessment, and Change Management Planning.

Mr. Goodwin has over 36 years of experience in Corporate Expansion, Mergers and Acquisitions, Income/Expense Management, and Execution Oversight. He has formed a team of professionals to offer actionable strategies to improve performance and sustain a lasting financial impact for growth. A key factor in his own success has been creating solutions for Managers, Owners and Investors to make well-informed decisions to address challenges and take advantage of opportunities.

During his 27 years with MUFG Union Bank, N.A., Mr. Goodwin elevated from Relationship Management to serving as Managing Director and Head of the Commercial Treasury Services Division within Transaction Banking

Americas. In this capacity, Goodwin was directly responsible for managing Deposit and Treasury-Services Strategy for a variety of segments, including Corporations, Middle Market, Business Banking, Non-Profit Businesses, Real Estate Developers/Investors, REIT Management Companies, and Commercial/Residential Property Management Companies. In 1987, Goodwin was appointed Acting President and Chief Executive Officer by the FDIC to manage daily operations and minimize loss exposure for a troubled financial institution. As a result of his involvement with the FDIC, Goodwin was hired in 1989 by Shearson Lehman Hutton as a Financial Consultant and Regional Institutional Salesperson to develop and structure securitization transactions for financial institutions in the Western region.

Goodwin has served on several committees and held board positions for the Los Angeles County Economic Development Corporation (LAEDC) and other associations, including the California Bankers Association and the Western Independent Bankers Association. Goodwin currently lives in Simi Valley, and keeps an office in Downtown Los Angeles.